HOW TO HANDLE MONEY

★ KIA COMMODORE ★

Published by Collins
An imprint of HarperCollins Publishers
Westerhill Road, Bishopbriggs,
Glasgow G64 2QT

HarperCollins Publishers
Macken House, 39/40 Mayor Street Upper,
Dublin 1, D01 C9W8, Ireland
harpercollins.co.uk

The contents of this publication are believed correct
at the time of printing. Nevertheless the publisher can
accept no responsibility for errors or omissions, changes
in the detail given or for any expense or loss thereby caused.

HarperCollins does not warrant that any website mentioned
in this title will be provided uninterrupted, that any website
will be error free, that defects will be corrected, or that
the website or the server that makes it available are free
of viruses or bugs. For full terms and conditions please
refer to the site terms provided on the website.

A catalogue record for this book is available
from the British Library.

978-0-00-869480-7

Printed in India by Replika Press Pvt. Ltd.
10 9 8 7 6 5 4 3 2 1

Publisher: Beth Ralston
Project Manager: Samuel Fitzgerald
Text Editing: Jess White, Elizabeth Fletcher
and Tony Michaelides
Design: Kevin Robbins
Typesetting: Simon Letchford
Production: Ilaria Rovera

CONTENTS

WELCOME TO *HOW TO HANDLE MONEY* – YOUR FIRST STEP TOWARDS TAKING CHARGE OF YOUR FINANCIAL FUTURE!

You might wonder, 'What's so difficult about money?' Money isn't just about buying things. It's what can help to make your dreams a reality, from allowing you to save for your first car to one day owning your own home. Having money doesn't automatically mean that it'll work hard for you. This requires something called money management, which is essentially **how to handle money** – how to save it, invest it and earn more of it are just a few of the things I'm here to show you. Here's exactly what you can expect from this book.

1. THE BASICS OF BUDGETING

I'll start off by introducing some core finance principles. Together, we'll explore the purpose of a savings budget and how to create your own, as well as different ways to save and earn interest. This will lay a solid foundation for your future financial planning.

2. THE ART OF SMART SPENDING

Next, I'll show you how to create a budget for spending, rather than saving. We'll look at the differences between cash and digital spending, the art of negotiating and how to ensure your payments are protected. I'll also share tips for earning extra money back on your purchases, setting financial goals and making informed financial decisions – so you can enjoy spending your money without blowing it all in one go!

3. THE DOS & DON'TS OF BORROWING

So far, we'll have talked about spending your own money, but here we'll learn about spending money that isn't yours – otherwise known as using credit. We'll break down credit history, credit checks and credit scores (things I wish I'd been taught sooner!). Then we'll cover manageable and unmanageable debt, so you can understand how to borrow responsibly.

4. KEEPING YOUR MONEY SAFE

We'll move on to the importance of online security. We'll talk about fraud and scams, and we'll look at how to spot the red flags so you can

prevent these things from affecting you. We'll also explore staying safe online with strong passwords, two-factor authentication and best practice for keeping your personal details and banking information secure. It can be hard to tell what's a scam and what's not so, if you have been a victim of a scam or know someone who has, we'll share some tips on how to navigate that.

5. INTRO TO INVESTING & RISK

Investing is a hot topic, but it can be hard to understand. We'll break down the different products you can invest in and how to choose the ones that fit your goals, values and risk appetite. We'll also explore how compound interest can boost your investments over time, as well as ways to avoid misleading financial content online and the temptation to gamble.

6. PLANNING FOR THE FUTURE

Finally, we'll look ahead at your bright and brilliant future! Are you going to go into further education? Are you beginning an apprenticeship, or kickstarting your career? Whichever path you

choose, this chapter covers everything you'll need to master your money in the long-term, including student finance, payslips, tax and pensions.

HOW TO USE THIS BOOK

Money is a big topic that can feel a bit overwhelming. What I want to emphasise here is that you don't need to feel the pressure to read this book from cover to cover when you first pick it up. See a chapter that you're particularly interested in? Jump straight in. This book is meant to be a tool, a guide that you can use to feel confident with money and finances. And with any good tool, each person is going to use it differently. So, read from Chapter 6 back to Chapter 1 or explore the chapters in random orders – however you choose to read it is entirely up to you. Make notes, highlight and scribble annotations. This book is yours to work and learn from.

At the end of each chapter you will see an 'action point'. These are here to reinforce what's been covered. Give each one a try, share them with friends and family and start those conversations. They're not there to test you so don't feel as though you need to get it 'right'; they're there so that you can begin to put into practice the things that you've learned.

I also recognise that we'll be covering a lot of new terms and complex concepts that might not always make sense the first time. Don't worry, the end of the book has a glossary of the key terms that you can flick to whenever you need. All of the terms that are featured in the glossary are in bold to help you spot them as you go.

So, whether you're looking to build on your financial knowledge or starting from the very beginning, this book will make sure that you're feeling confident with your finances and ready to take control of your future.

READY? LET'S GET STARTED!

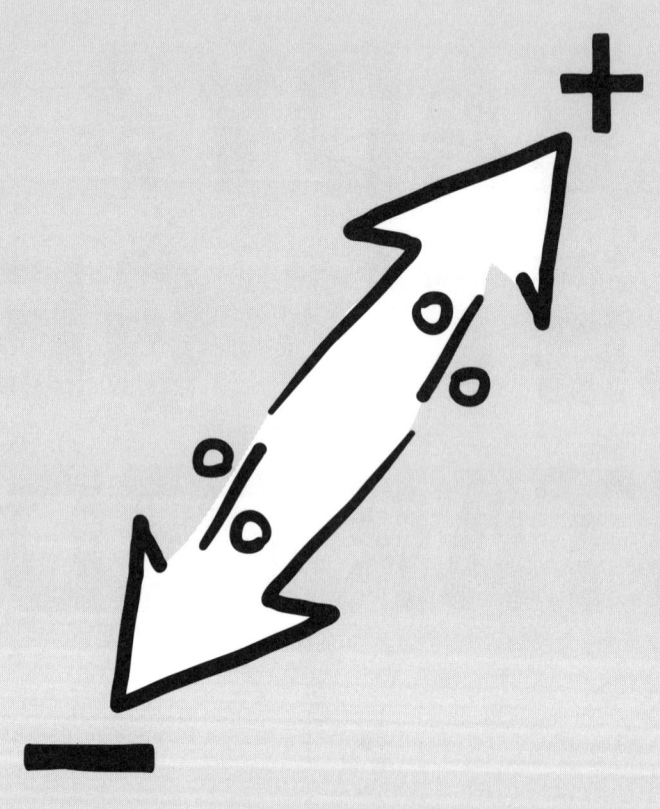

1 THE BASICS OF BUDGETING

LET'S DIVE STRAIGHT INTO THE EXCITING WORLD OF MONEY AND TALK ABOUT SAVING...

Imagine you've just got your first job. You've been working shifts in a clothing store or a restaurant and are eagerly anticipating a proper chunk of money that you earned by yourself. Then, you finally receive it – your first paycheck. Your brain is running at a hundred miles an hour thinking of all the things that you could buy with that money. Clothes, trainers, the latest phone (maybe after a few more paychecks!) – the list seems endless. You go home and tell your family that you're officially rich (well, it feels like that anyway) and they tell you that it's important to budget your money before splashing all your cash.

So, what now?

BUDGETING

BUDGETING FOR SAVING

Before you can decide how much money you're going to put away into **savings,** you first need to create something called a **budget.** A budget is a plan of where and how much of your money is going to be spent. As you get older, you will find that there are things that just must be paid for – such as electricity, water, gas, phone use, etc. These need to be paid for to be able to live and maintain a lifestyle, so this is called **necessary spending.**

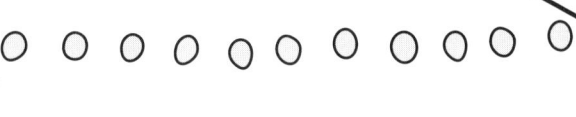

INCOME

This is how much money you have coming in, for example pocket money or a wage from your part-time job.

OUTGOINGS

These are what you plan to spend your money on and include your necessary spending.

DEBT

This is money you've borrowed that needs to be paid back, for example a loan (you'll learn more about debt in Chapter 3).

SAVINGS

This is how much you plan to save.

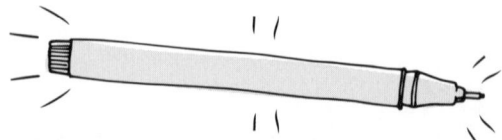

Your budget doesn't need to be fancy or complicated. You can use a pen and paper to create the different categories and jot down the numbers for your budget. Alternatively, if you're confident with your computer skills, creating a budget using a spreadsheet program will make it easier for you to make edits to your **income** and **outgoings** over time.

HERE'S AN EXAMPLE OF A SIMPLE BUDGET:

It's helpful to create a budget each month or every time you receive money, so you have a good idea of where your money is going. As in the example on the right, you might find you have a bit extra left over to either save or spend!

CATEGORY	AMOUNT
INCOME	
part-time job	£200
OUTGOINGS	
mobile phone bill	£15
cinema trip	£25
DEBT	
student overdraft repayment	£50
SAVINGS	
emergency fund	£40
new trainers	£10
TOTAL INCOME	£200
TOTAL OUTGOINGS	£140
REMAINDER	£60

SAVINGS

THE 50/30/20 RULE

The 50/30/20 rule gives a general idea of how much of your money you should put into different budget categories. The breakdown goes like this:

50% of your money should go towards your needs, for example bills

30% of your money should go towards your wants, for example new clothes and eating out

20% of your money should go towards your savings.

For example, if you have £50, you might choose to put 20% of that into savings (£10). If you're under 18, it's unlikely that you'll have many bills to pay, so you could use the remaining £40 to spend on things that you want.

WHY SHOULD I SAVE?

Saving is when you put some of your money aside, ideally into a separate savings pot or account, so that you can spend it in the future. For example, if you get £10 for your birthday, you might choose to put £2 into savings (to spend later) and keep the remaining £8 (to spend now).

But why would you want to set aside some money when you could just enjoy spending it all? There are a few reasons, such as:

★ to buy something that you really want but don't have enough money for just yet, such as a pair of shoes

★ in case of an emergency, for example if you accidentally break your phone and need to pay to get it fixed

★ for a future goal, for example you might have a dream of going to university and want to put some money aside for when that day comes.

DREAM BIG

INTEREST

WHAT IS INTEREST?

Another reason to save some of your money is to earn **interest** over time. When you save your money in a bank account – depending on how much is in there and how long you leave it there for – the bank gives you something called interest. Let's say that you have £10 in your savings. Your friend asks to borrow that money for one month and, after that, they promise to give it straight back. You say yes and give it to them because you don't need the money right now. One month flies by and your friend returns your £10 but gives you an extra 15p on top as a thank you. That 15p is the interest that you've earned on your savings. Banks pay out interest in the same way.

HOW DOES INTEREST WORK?

When you have money in a savings account, the bank lends your savings out to different customers as loans, for example to buy a car or a house. But don't panic! Although this might sound worrying, your money is completely protected. Every regulated bank and financial provider in the UK is covered by the Financial Services Compensation Scheme (FSCS). This means that money held in a UK bank account is covered up to the value of £85,000 for a single account or £170,000 for a joint account. If the bank loses money and goes bust, you're guaranteed to get your money back up to those values. If you're fortunate enough to have more than £85,000 of personal savings, you may want to think about separating your savings across more than one bank account to protect your money.

Each month or year,
the bank adds interest on top of your
savings as a thank you. This is also known
as a reward for saving. So, the more money
you have in a savings account, the more interest
you're likely to earn. The amount of interest that you'll
earn is typically shown as a percentage, for example
2% **AER (annual equivalent rate).** Put simply, this is the
percentage of interest that you will earn on your savings
each year and it accounts for the interest that you might
earn on your savings. So, if you have £100 in savings and
leave it in the savings account for a year, you would
earn 2% interest on top, giving you a total of £102
at the end of that year. (You'll learn more
about compound interest in
Chapter5.)

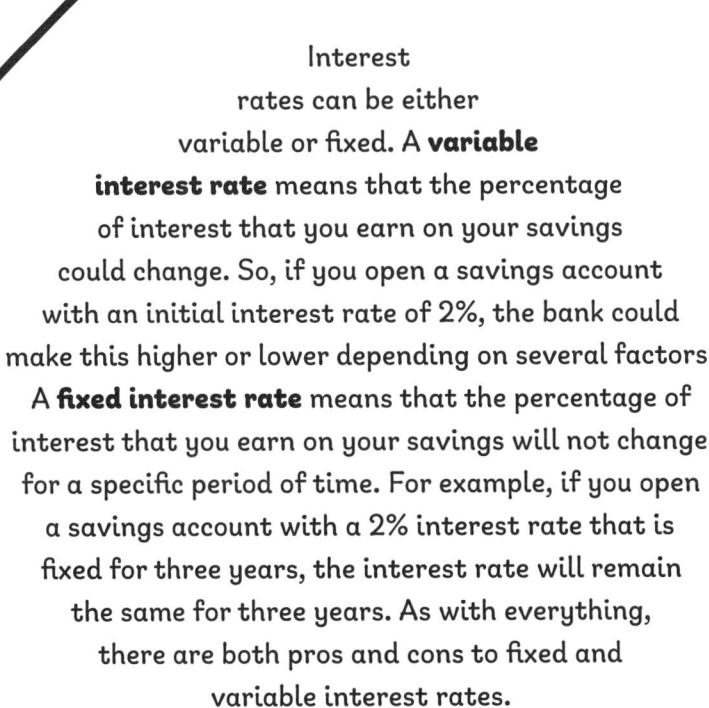

Interest
rates can be either
variable or fixed. A **variable
interest rate** means that the percentage
of interest that you earn on your savings
could change. So, if you open a savings account
with an initial interest rate of 2%, the bank could
make this higher or lower depending on several factors.
A **fixed interest rate** means that the percentage of
interest that you earn on your savings will not change
for a specific period of time. For example, if you open
a savings account with a 2% interest rate that is
fixed for three years, the interest rate will remain
the same for three years. As with everything,
there are both pros and cons to fixed and
variable interest rates.

VARIABLE INTEREST RATES

☑ <u>PROS</u>

☑ When interest rates are increased in the economy, you can benefit from these increases and earn a higher reward on your savings.

☑ When it comes to choosing a savings account with a variable rate, there is often a lot more choice, so you can pick the account that suits you best.

☑ Savings accounts with variable rates tend to have more flexibility so you're able to withdraw money as and when you need with little to no restrictions.

☒ <u>CONS</u>

☒ Just as the interest rate can increase, it can also fall. This means that you could earn a lower reward on your savings.

☒ Because the interest rates can change, it can be harder to accurately plan your financial goals and know how much your money could grow.

☒ You could potentially be earning a lower rate of interest on your savings compared to a fixed rate account.

FIXED INTEREST RATES

 PROS

☑ The interest rate tends to be higher compared to variable rates due to how the account works.

☑ Because the rate is fixed, you're able to plan your finances and know exactly how much you'll be earning.

☑ Fixed rate accounts typically have limited access when it comes to withdrawing your money, so you're able to save and let your money grow without being tempted to dip in.

 CONS

☒ If you need to access your money in a fixed rate account before the end of the fixed term, you may have to pay a fee.

☒ If interest rates rise, you won't be able to benefit from the increase as your interest rate is set.

☒ Some fixed rate accounts have a minimum amount that you need to deposit to open the account.

☒ Most fixed rate accounts do not allow you to add to your savings during the fixed period, so you would need to have all the money that you're looking to deposit ready before opening the account.

SO WHERE SHOULD I SAVE MY MONEY?

Now you understand the importance of saving and how interest works, where are the different places that you can put your money?

MONEY BOX

This is a pot or jar for storing coins and notes that you'll likely have at home. Growing up, I had several different money boxes – one shaped like a pig, another like a dinosaur and even an electronic box that would reel in bank notes like a cash machine. The shape and style are totally up to you, but it's always useful to have a money box to pop in some of your loose change and get into the habit of saving. However, you may want to upgrade to a savings account once you start earning a regular income (for example your first job) so you can start earning interest too.

CURRENT ACCOUNT

A current account is likely to be the first type of bank account you open. It is not a type of savings account but instead is where you'll receive any incoming money (such as wages) and where you'll do your day-to-day spending. Current accounts offer little to no interest, as they're not designed for money to be saved in, but they're necessary for organising and spending your money.

EASY ACCESS SAVINGS ACCOUNT

This is an account that you can open at a bank (with the help of an adult if you're under the age of 16 – which is also true for the rest of the accounts in this list) that allows you to put in and take out money whenever you wish. This is generally the most flexible savings account. However, because of this, this account usually has a lower interest rate.

NOTICE SAVINGS ACCOUNT

This is an account that you can open at the bank that allows you to save money whenever you would like to. The only difference between this and an easy access savings account is that you need to let the bank know whenever you plan to take some of your savings out of the account (also known as giving notice). The amount of notice that you must give depends on which account you open, but it is usually between one and three months' notice. So, what's the benefit of this account? Typically, this account has a higher interest rate *because* you're not able to take out your money instantly.

FIXED RATE SAVINGS ACCOUNT

This is an account that you can open at the bank where the interest rate is fixed for a certain time period. You can only put money into this savings account one time, which means you need to have all your savings ready when you open it. After that, the savings are locked away for a fixed time period, which means you're not allowed to take any money out until that time is up. If you need to take out money earlier, you may have to pay a fine (which is why it's important to decide how much money you want to put into this account). The benefit of this account is that it usually has a much higher interest rate compared to other savings accounts.

JUNIOR ISA

This stands for 'individual savings account', and is an account that allows you to save money whenever you'd like to. The benefit of this account is that you do not pay tax on interest earned from the account. That sentence probably had you saying 'huh, what does that mean?'. To explain it simply, when you earn and spend money, you'll often have to give a part of that money to the government in taxes. When it comes to your savings, you may have to give a portion of the interest that you earn as tax. With the junior ISA, no tax is paid on the interest from your savings up to the amount of £9,000 in the UK. So, if you don't save more than this each year (in the UK this is each tax year, meaning April–April; this varies in different parts of the world), you won't have to pay any tax on interest earned. Also, your money is locked away and cannot be taken out until you reach the age of 18. Like all ISAs, Junior ISAs come in two forms, 'cash' or 'stocks and shares'.

JUNIOR CASH ISA: This is very similar to a normal savings account where you're able to deposit money and earn interest on your savings.

JUNIOR STOCKS AND SHARES ISA: This is a bit different as, instead of just sitting in the bank, any savings in this account are invested into other companies through something called the stock market. By investing your savings, you might earn even more than you would from interest alone and your money can grow. However, this can be riskier as you may get back less savings than you originally put in. (You'll learn more about investing in Chapter 5.)

CAN I ONLY HAVE ONE TYPE OF SAVINGS ACCOUNT?

As we've just explored, there are many types of savings accounts that work in different ways to help your money grow. It can be useful to have a few different types of savings accounts because this lets you split your savings into various goals. For example, one account could be dedicated to building your emergency fund and another could be for saving towards your first holiday with friends. Separating out your savings is a great way to keep track of how close you are to reaching your savings goals.

You can also benefit from having more than one ISA. The two different types of junior ISAs were mentioned earlier, but there are other ISAs that you could open depending on your financial goals once you're over 18:

STOCKS AND SHARES ISA

Like the junior stocks and shares ISA, this account allows you to invest the money that you save into the stock market through investment funds. This account has a saving limit of £20,000 per tax year.

CASH ISA

Like the junior cash ISA, this account allows you to save money and earn interest on your savings. This account also has a limit of £20,000 per tax year.

LIFETIME ISA (LISA)

This is a type of ISA that allows you to save money towards your first home or for retirement. You can save a maximum of £4,000 per tax year and the government will top up those savings with a 25% bonus (£1,000 maximum) each tax year. You can choose to make it a cash LISA or a stocks and shares LISA.

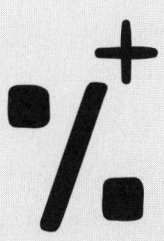

The great thing about ISAs is you're able to have one of each type per tax year. The £20,000 tax-free limit can be split across all the ISAs that you hold, allowing you to grow your money in various pots tax-free. How you choose to split the limit is completely up to you. For example, you could split it like this:

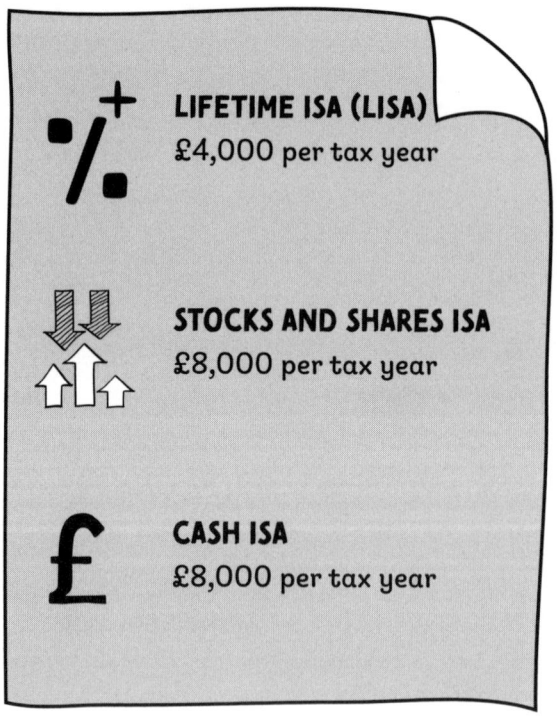

LIFETIME ISA (LISA)
£4,000 per tax year

STOCKS AND SHARES ISA
£8,000 per tax year

CASH ISA
£8,000 per tax year

HOW MUCH SHOULD I SAVE?

Saving, along with everything else that you'll learn within this book, falls under a massive umbrella topic called personal finance. What's the first word there? *Personal.* That means, when it comes to making decisions about your money, it's all down to you. How much you choose to save may not be the same as your sibling, friend or cousin because it all depends on how much money you have and your reasons for saving. Even though there isn't a specific amount to follow, it can help to follow some simple guidelines. We mentioned the 50/30/20 rule earlier, and another similar guide is the 70/30 rule. This rule suggests that you use 70% of your income to cover living expenses and other outgoings, and the remaining 30% is split up across your savings (investments included) and donating to charity.

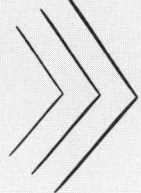

✓ How to create a budget

✓ The importance of savings

✓ What interest rates are and the different types

✓ Different places to put your money

✓ The benefits of having more than one savings account

✓ How to work out how much to save

ACTION POINT

Want to put what you've learned into action?
Here's an activity to try.

Think about your next big purchase – this could
be a new game, clothes or a phone. Create a
savings plan using the templates over the page
to work out how long it'll take you to reach your
goal amount.

What I want to buy:

How much it will cost me:

When I want to buy it:

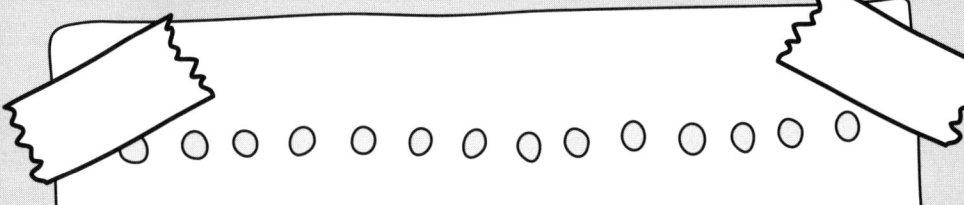

Savings plan

Month 1:

Month 4:

Month 2:

Month 5:

Month 3:

Month 6:

2 THE ART OF SMART SPENDING

WHAT NEXT?

In Chapter 1, you learned about saving and why it's important to put some of your money away towards a goal or 'just in case'. In this chapter, you'll learn about the other 's' – spending!

You've received your first paycheck, created your budget, paid your bills and set aside some of your money for your savings goals. Now you've got some money left over and you want to spend, spend, spend – you've worked hard for your money so you can enjoy a good shopping trip!

When it comes to spending, there are two ways that you can go about things:

1.

SPLASH THE CASH WITH NO IDEA HOW MUCH YOU'VE SPENT AND ON WHAT.

2.

PLAN YOUR SPENDING AND KNOW WHAT YOU CAN AFFORD TO BUY.

Shopping budget

If you haven't already guessed, I'm going to champion the second approach. So, with that said, let's break down how to plan your spending.

SPENDING

BUDGETING FOR SPENDING

You learned about budgeting for saving in Chapter 1, but it's just as important to create a budget for your spending. By creating a plan for your spending, you can make your money last longer and buy the things that you really want.

HERE'S AN EXAMPLE OF A SPENDING BUDGET:

A spending budget is very similar to the budget you saw in Chapter 1. The difference is that the items in this budget are things that you want to buy.

A spending budget gives you a clear plan of what you're going to spend your money on, how much things cost and how long your money will last you.

CATEGORY	AMOUNT
INCOME REMAINDER	£60
SPENDING	
new trousers	£25
Jessica's birthday dinner	£20
new top	£10
bus pass	£3
TOTAL AVAILABLE	£60

TOTAL SPENDING $\qquad$ £58

CASH VS DIGITAL SPENDING?

Although for a long time only cash was used for everyday spending, in the UK almost everything is now digital. Bank accounts are online and can be accessed on our phones, and money can be transferred in minutes. Apps such as Apple Pay and Google Pay can store a virtual equivalent of any credit or debit card, reducing the need even to carry those when you're out shopping, let alone cash. There has also been a massive shift to online shopping in recent years.

Think back to the last five things that you bought. How did you pay for them – with cash or using your phone? Perhaps you shopped online. When I think about how I pay for things day-to-day, almost all the time I'm tapping my phone on the card machine. Digital spending has a lot of pros:

☑ You can check out in minutes.

☑ You can shop from the comfort of your own home.

☑ You can transfer money between accounts in seconds.

☑ You can approve and verify purchases straight from your devices.

Digital spending is very convenient, but it can make it easier to spend, spend, spend! The ease of being able to pay by just tapping your phone or entering a few card details can sometimes lead you to part with more money than you planned.

On the flip side, you have good old cash. There is much less demand for coins and notes in shops than there used to be, with some shops being exclusively card only, but cash still has its pros:

☑ You can budget easily and only spend the cash that you physically have.

☑ There are no extra fees when paying with cash.

☑ It can be useful when buying things that are low cost (for example a bus ticket).

VS

NEGOTIATION

It's likely that most of your spending will be done digitally. However, you never know when you might need to make a quick purchase and some small shops may not have card facilities. Having cash in hand can be useful at times, but try not to leave the house with large amounts on you as that can make you vulnerable to theft. It's important to note that if you're paying using a contactless card the spending limit is £100 but there is no limit when paying using Apple Pay or Google Pay.

WHAT IS NEGOTIATION?

As you navigate life and begin paying for more things – such as phone bills, car insurance and the general costs that come with being an adult – there's one skill that is key to learn: negotiating.

Growing up, I have many memories of being on holiday with my family. My dad would try to negotiate the prices of items whenever we were at local markets. At the time, I didn't understand why, because I always assumed that you had to pay whatever price you'd been told when you're looking to buy things. Then, as I got older, I realised that this isn't always the case.

HOW TO NEGOTIATE

To put it simply, **negotiation** (also known as haggling or bargaining) is a discussion between two parties (for example between two people or between a person and a company) to reach a decision that both sides agree on. So, putting this into the context of the market, negotiation is when my dad says what he wants to pay for an item, the stallholder says what they want to receive for it and they discuss this until they agree a price that they are both happy with.

Day-to-day, you won't find yourself negotiating the prices of regular items in the supermarket or the price of your favourite shoes at the shop because those are set prices. Even if these items are on sale, the price isn't in your control.

However, there are a few things that you can negotiate prices on, including:

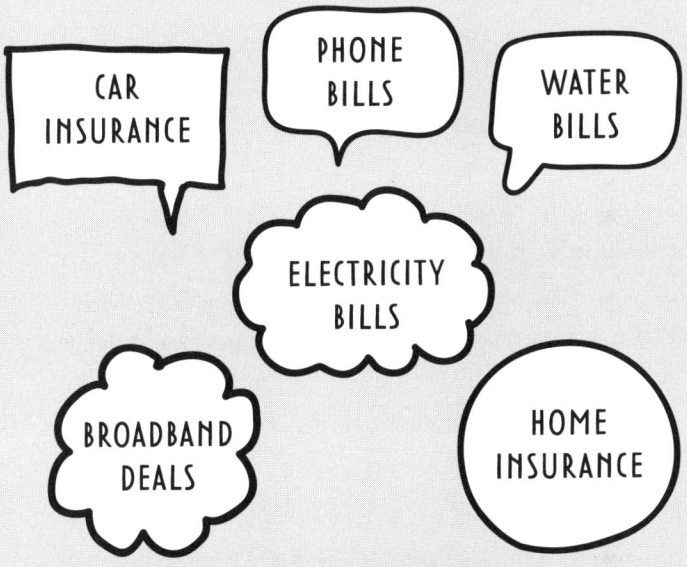

CAR INSURANCE

PHONE BILLS

WATER BILLS

ELECTRICITY BILLS

BROADBAND DEALS

HOME INSURANCE

And the list goes on. When shopping for items or services like these, you can often have a conversation (usually over the phone or via a live web chat) to see if you can get a lower price than the one that you are first told. You're also able to **renegotiate** when it is time to renew your **contract** so you're not stuck paying the same price (or even more) forever.

PROTECTION

PROTECTION WHEN MAKING PURCHASES

Shopping is great when the items or services that you've purchased work and there are no issues. But, what happens when things go wrong? What happens when an item that you've bought turns out to be broken once you get it home? This is where **purchase protection** comes in.

Purchase protection is cover that is given to you when you purchase goods (AKA items) or services. The level of protection that you get depends on how you make the payment.

CASH

When you pay with cash, there's pretty much no extra protection on your purchases apart from the **statutory rights** that you're entitled to as a consumer. These are the basic legal rights that every consumer has *not* to be sold an item or service that doesn't work or isn't as described. If anything goes wrong with your purchase that falls outside of these rights, retailers are not required to give you a refund or replacement. If you make a purchase using cash, ensure that you keep your receipt as proof of your purchase in case you need to return a faulty item.

DEBIT CARD

In addition to your statutory rights as a consumer, when you pay with a **debit card** you may be entitled to a **chargeback** if something goes wrong with a purchase, such as if an item is damaged or faulty. A chargeback is when a payment is given back to a customer after they have been successful in a dispute (similar to making a complaint) for an item on their bank transaction history. This is done directly through your bank.

A chargeback is not mandatory. It's up to the bank to decide whether they agree with the argument that you submit in your dispute. You must explain what the issue is and why you're looking to get a refund. As part of your dispute, the bank will ask you to give them evidence, such as proof of purchase, any pictures (if the item is faulty or damaged) and any proof of communications if you have tried to get in contact with the retailer.

CREDIT CARD

Like with a debit card, you may be entitled to a refund or replacement of an item if you make a payment using a **credit card**. This is a legal right that you have as a credit card holder under Section 75 of the **Consumer Credit Act**. Put simply, this act means that, should anything go wrong, the credit card company is jointly responsible with the retailer to fix any issues with your purchase (for any purchases between £100 and £30,000).

So, if you use your credit card to buy a new laptop and it arrives broken, and the retailer refuses to replace it or give you a refund, your credit card company is also responsible and must find a resolution for your problem.

BARGAINS

COMPARISON SHOPPING

You might not be able to negotiate the prices of regular household items, but there are still ways that you can save money when you're shopping. One example is through **comparison shopping**.

HOW DOES COMPARISON SHOPPING WORK?

The most important factor when it comes to comparison shopping is to make sure you compare the price of an item across many different shops and retailers. If you're looking to buy something that is expensive like a phone or TV, it is worth doing your research and comparing prices first.

Now, you can compare the price of an item
the old-fashioned way – by navigating to
each website or walking round different
shops to see which one offers the lowest price.
However, thanks to the power of technology,
there are several websites and apps that
will do the hard work for you. Websites like
Trolley allow you to compare the prices of
many household items – such as food, beauty
items and electronics – across all the different
supermarkets and other retailers. This makes it
easy to find out which shop has the best prices
for the items that you're looking to buy.

It's particularly important to comparison shop
ahead of 'sale' events like Black Friday and
Cyber Monday. Many shops can be a bit cheeky
by raising the prices of items before these events
and then lowering them on Black Friday/Cyber
Monday to make it seem like you're getting a
discount when, in reality, you're probably not.

1. A week before the sale is due to start, make a list of the items that you'd like to buy and how much they currently cost. This helps you see how much the items cost before the sale begins and gives you something to compare prices to.

2. On the sale days, either visit shops (online or in person) or use price comparison tools to compare the sale prices of your items against the original prices from the week before.

3. Check if there are any extra discounts that you could use, such as a student discount or promotional code. These can help to bring those prices down even further.

4. Once you've found the best price for the item that you're looking to buy, go ahead and check out!

CASHBACK

Another way of saving money when shopping, besides looking for discounts or negotiating, is **cashback.** Growing up, the only time I heard the term 'cashback' was when my parents were at the supermarket checkout and the cashier would ask if they wanted cashback. This was simply using the supermarket till like a cash machine, where you could 'withdraw' up to around £50 in cash by adding it to your total before paying for your shopping with your bank card. However, cashback has another meaning.

Cashback is just what it sounds like – a way for you to get cash back on your purchases. Getting money back when you're spending money almost sounds too good to be true, doesn't it? Well, rest assured that this is in fact true and there are a few websites and apps that allow you to earn cashback while spending money.

HOW DOES CASHBACK WORK?

Let's imagine that you have a friend who runs a clothes shop. Your friend tells you that for every time you bring someone to their shop and they buy an item, your friend will give you a percentage of the money they make as a thank you. So, what do you do? You go out and spread the word to bring people to your friend's shop so that, in return, you'll get a cut of what each person spends.

This is how cashback websites and apps work – they're the go-between for you (the consumer) and the place where you're shopping (the retailer). The only difference is, they decide to share a portion of their cut with you, the

consumer, as a thank you and to encourage you to continue shopping through them. Because cashback websites and apps make their money through the shops and brands, these services are often free for you to use and earn money from. Some apps can also make additional income through showing you ads and sometimes through selling customer data. Be sure to read the fine print whenever you're signing up to a cashback site (and when online in general) to understand how your personal information is going to be used.

Some banks offer cashback to their customers through their banking apps (depending on the type of account you have) as an additional perk for being a customer. There are also popular websites such as Quidco and TopCashback that list a wide range of shops that you can earn cashback from. Most of these cashback services require you to be over the age of 16, so make sure to check the age restrictions before you sign up.

1. Visit the cashback app or website of your choice.

2. Search for the retailer that you're looking to buy from and click on the website through the cashback site.

3. You'll be taken to the retailer's website. You need to go to the cashback site first so that your purchase can be tracked and the site will know how much cashback you'll earn. (You don't need to worry too much about how this works, just know that this step is essential so you can earn your money.)

4. Shop as normal!

5. After you've finished shopping and made your payment, you'll get a notification (usually via email) letting you know how much cashback you've earned on your purchase.

6. After a period of time (it could be a few months or even up to a year), cashback will be added to your cashback account. You can withdraw that money either straight into your bank account or onto a gift card of your choosing.

Cashback is a no-brainer when it comes to your spending. It's a way to earn money while spending it – what's better than that? As always, it's important to mention that this shouldn't be a reason to spend more than you need to. Tools such as cashback are a useful bonus when you're buying things, but they shouldn't encourage **overspending**. Plan your spending first and use cashback only on your pre-planned purchases.

MAKING INFORMED DECISIONS

This chapter has covered many different topics related to spending money – budgeting for your purchases, negotiating your bills and comparing prices of items. Although spending can be great fun and is often an essential part of your money management, it is important to be in control and make informed financial decisions.

GOALS

FINANCIAL GOALS

While this book is here to help you learn what you can do with your money, it is equally important to know the reasons *why* you're doing these things. As you learned in Chapter 1, having financial goals can give you a blueprint for what to do with your money that will benefit future you! They can help you to:

 decide what you're going to do with your money (for example spend, save or invest)

 create a timeline of how long it's going to take to reach your goal (for example if your goal is to go on holiday, you can work out when you can go by knowing how long it'll take you to save the amount you need)

 make decisions today that will benefit future you financially (for example only buying takeaway once or twice a month so you can put some extra money into savings).

Another practice that I started in my teens to help me make good financial decisions was creating a spending journal. A spending journal is where you can keep track of all your spending decisions. It's similar to a budget but looks back. In this journal, you can note how much you've spent on things, why you bought them and how they made you feel.

Detailing your spending in this way will give you a clear picture of your spending habits and may highlight areas that you can cut back on if you find yourself overspending. This is a good habit to get into early, even if you're only earning a small amount from pocket money or working part-time. It will give you the necessary skills to manage your income when you get your first full-time job.

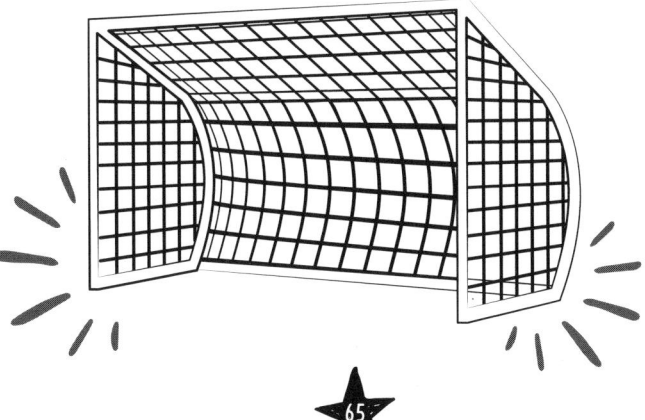

✓ How to create a budget for your spending

✓ The pros and cons of cash vs digital spending

✓ What negotiation is

✓ How to qualify for purchase protection

✓ How to compare prices when shopping

✓ What cashback is

✓ Ways to make informed financial decisions

ACTION POINT

Want to put what you've learned into action? Here's an activity to try.

For the next week, keep your own spending journal. You can write this journal in a notebook or on the notes app on your smartphone if you have one. The example is in paragraph format, but you could also bullet point your key spending for your spending journal.

Example spending journal

Saturday 14th June

Items bought:

- ☑ Lunch with friends (£12)

- ☑ New jumper (£15)

- ☑ Pretzels (£3.50)

- ☑ Total = £30.50

Today, I went to my local shopping centre to spend the day with my friends. I hadn't eaten all day, so I got a burger meal with a large milkshake that came to £12 but I didn't finish it all.

I've wanted this jumper for a while and it had recently gone on sale for £15, so this was a great purchase. I'm super happy with it!

Because we'd been walking around for a few hours, I got a big bit hungry. I decided to stop by the pretzel stand and bought some pretzel sticks for £3.50.

Overall, it was a good spending day today! My one takeaway is that I'm going to be realistic with how much I can eat and perhaps see if there's a slightly cheaper food option to go for when I'm out with my friends.

NOW WRITE YOUR OWN.
AT THE END OF THE WEEK, WRITE:

★ One thing that you did well with your spending:

_____

_____

_____

_____

_____

_____

★ One thing that you'd like to improve with your spending:

_____

_____

_____

_____

_____

3 THE DOS & DON'TS OF BORROWING

CREDIT

In the last two chapters, you have learned about how to manage your money – from budgeting and saving to understanding how much you're spending and why you're spending it. In this chapter, you'll learn about money that's not *actually* yours. Before you panic, this is nothing illegal! This is borrowing money using something called **credit**.

WHAT IS CREDIT?

Credit is an agreement where one party (the bank or a financial institution) agrees to lend money to another party (in this case, you as the consumer) knowing that this money is going to be paid back at some point in the future.

The most common form of **borrowing** you may have heard of is a **credit card**. A credit card is similar to a debit card (though it's only available to people aged 18 and over), but it allows the owner to buy items on credit, i.e. before you actually have the money in your account.

THERE ARE ALSO OTHER FORMS OF BORROWING, SUCH AS:

 **A PERSONAL LOAN** – a lump sum of money that can be used towards a purchase of your choice (for example to renovate your house)

 **AN OVERDRAFT** – a small buffer of credit that lets you withdraw more money than you have in your account

 **A MORTGAGE** – a large lump sum used to purchase a property (for example your first house)

 **CAR FINANCE** – a lump sum offered by a car dealership to purchase a car

 A STUDENT LOAN – a loan given to students to cover their study costs (tuition fees) and/or living costs (maintenance loan).

1. split the cost of a big purchase over a period of time (for example you could pay for the item in full over six months)

2. protect your purchase in case your item breaks or stops working. In the UK, this is under a law called Section 75 of the Consumer Credit Act (you don't need to worry about this too much – all you need to know is that if you use a credit card to buy something worth between £100 and £30,000, the credit card company is there to help you if anything goes wrong with that item)

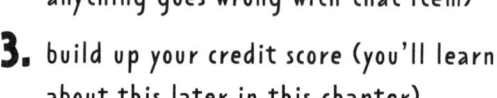

3. build up your credit score (you'll learn about this later in this chapter)

4. have a financial cushion to fall back on (for example if you're waiting for payday but you need to replace the broken screen on your phone before then, you can use credit to pay now and pay it back as soon as you get paid)

Credit is a useful finance tool when used correctly but it's important to highlight that it is not free money. This money must be paid back and, often, the repayment is higher than the amount of money you borrowed in the first place. This is because of interest. Remember that from Chapter 1? Here's a refresher.

WHAT HAVE YOU LEARNED ABOUT INTEREST SO FAR?

When it comes to saving, interest is the 'reward' that you get for saving. The bank uses your money while it's sitting in your account to lend it to other customers in the form of loans, overdrafts and so on, to make more money. As a 'thank you', they pay you a percentage on top of your savings in the form of interest.

WHAT IS INTEREST WHEN IT COMES TO CREDIT?

When it comes to credit, interest works in reverse. Rather than a reward, credit interest is the charge that you pay to lenders for borrowing money. With a credit card, you won't need to pay any interest on the amount that you've borrowed if you repay the credit card in full within an agreed time frame. This is typically a month but can vary depending on the lender. If you don't repay the full amount within that time frame, interest charges may be added.

> Let's say that you borrow **£50** from the bank through an overdraft. If the overdraft charges **20%** interest on any amount that is borrowed, this means that you'll have to repay the initial **£50** that you borrowed plus **20%** interest (which is **£10**), making the total to pay back **£60**.

Interest charges are typically added to any borrowed amount that you haven't paid back on a monthly basis. So, if you don't repay all the money that you've borrowed the following month, additional interest will be added.

This is where something called **compound interest** kicks in.

Compound interest is when there is interest added on top of interest. To explain this, let's go back to the example above.

You initially borrow **£50** from your overdraft in month one. The **20%** interest is added to the **£50** (because you haven't paid it back in full yet), making your total to pay back **£60**. In month two, the **20%** interest will be calculated on the **£60** (your borrowed **£50** + **£10** interest), making your month two total **£72** (**£60** + **£12** interest).

Compound interest can make borrowing very costly if you don't have a solid repayment plan.

Whenever you borrow any money, it is important to look at the interest rate that is going to be charged. The higher the interest rate, the more money you'll have to repay. Before you apply for any credit card, overdraft or other form of credit you will be told what the interest rate is *likely* to be. However, that rate isn't guaranteed because the interest rate that you are given depends on your **credit history**.

WHAT IS A CREDIT HISTORY?

A credit history is a record of how you've used credit in the past. It's like a journal that keeps track of your credit use, such as:

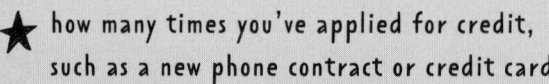 how many times you've applied for credit, such as a new phone contract or credit card

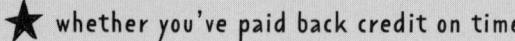 whether you've paid back credit on time

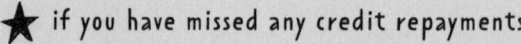 if you have missed any credit repayments

if you have any strikes on your credit file, for example **county court judgments** or a default (more on these later in this chapter).

If your credit history shows that you're not very responsible with credit – for example by not making repayments on your credit card on time – you might be given a higher interest rate by a lender when you come to apply for credit. This is because you will be seen as a higher-risk

borrower. Put simply, the lender is not sure whether they will get back all the money that they loan to you. The costs can add up for the lender to try to get that money back through sending letters, agents to visit your home and, if it gets that far, going to court.

So, this potential cost is passed on to you, the borrower, and the lender charges you more interest on the money you have borrowed compared to someone who has a better credit history. Or they might refuse to lend the money at all. This is why it's important to make sure that, when you're old enough and ready to start using credit, you use it responsibly and have a solid plan to repay the money.

In the UK, there are three main credit reference agencies: TransUnion, Experian and Equifax. A credit reference agency is a company that keeps a record of your credit history and, based on that, gives you something called a **credit score**. A credit score is a number that shows how responsible you are at borrowing money. So, the higher your credit score, the more responsible you're seen to be by companies who lend money.

WANT TO KNOW WHAT YOUR CREDIT SCORE IS?

All the credit reference agencies let you check your credit score for free, either online or by sending a paper copy to your home address. It's important to highlight that each credit reference agency will give you a different credit score. This is because each agency takes into consideration the factors that make up your credit score in different percentages. No matter which agency you use, there are ways to build up your credit score (once you're over 18 years old):

PAY YOUR CREDIT CARD BILL, PHONE BILL AND OTHER BORROWING-RELATED BILLS ON TIME – this shows lenders that you're responsible, borrowing money and paying it back when it's due.

PAY YOUR CREDIT CARD IN FULL – whenever you can, paying all your credit card back in one go means that you won't have to pay back extra in interest, and shows that you can be trusted t o borrow money.

BE ON THE ELECTORAL ROLL – this means making sure that you're registered to vote (what age you can register depends on where in the UK you live). When it comes to credit, being registered to vote lets lenders double-check that you are who you say you are.

When you apply for credit, there are two different types of checks that can be done on your credit file by the bank or lender: soft checks and hard checks. Each of these checks can affect your credit score in different ways.

SOFT CHECK

Soft checks happen when you do searches on a comparison site for things such as car insurance, phone contracts or home insurance. This is also the type of check that is done when you check your own credit score. This only checks basic information such as your name, age, address and overall borrowing history, and it doesn't affect your credit score.

HARD CHECK

A hard check happens when you apply for a new form of credit, such as a credit card, overdraft or phone contract. The potential lender will want to find out further details on your credit file, such as your existing loans, how good you are at repaying credit and how long you've been borrowing money for. Hard checks are visible on your credit file, so if you make lots of unsuccessful applications this could negatively impact your credit score.

DEBT

You don't need to worry too much about the differences between the two checks, but it's important to know how they work and how they could potentially impact your credit score. For instance, it's a bad idea to apply for credit that you are unlikely to be approved for, as this rejection can make it even harder to get approved for future loans. Check your credit score in advance to help you avoid this situation.

CREDIT FILE STRIKES

A strike or mark on your credit file is when you've missed or failed to repay credit that you've borrowed. This is noted on your credit file and impacts your credit score. It could be any of the following:

A missed/late payment is when you have either missed the payment date to make the minimum repayment or have paid after that date, which is seen as a late payment.

A county court judgment (or CCJ for short) is applied for by the lender if they think that you won't repay the money that you owe them. If the courts agree with the lender, they will issue a ruling that demands that you repay the money that is owed.

A **default** is when a lender chooses to completely close your credit account because you have missed too many payments. This is usually if you've missed payments for the last three to six months, but this depends on the terms that you've agreed with the lender. Any money that is still owed will need to be repaid in full by the date given to you by the lender.

Any strikes on your credit file will remain there for six years (even if all the money owed has been paid back) and will be seen by lenders every time you apply for a new form of credit and a hard search is done. This negatively impacts your credit score, though the effect decreases the closer you get to the end of the six years.

MANAGEABLE VS UNMANAGEABLE DEBT

When you hear the word **'debt'** it is often framed as a bad thing. This is not always the case as debt can fall into two different categories.

Interest is charged on the money that is borrowed (as well as other fees such as a late payment fee) ↓

Borrowing more money to repay what was initially borrowed.

Borrowing money to pay for items →

Not repaying the money on time/not having enough money to repay ↑

Manageable debt is when the borrower has created a budget to repay and has a regular income to cover this cost.

Unmanageable debt is when the borrower has taken out more than they can afford and does not have a plan to repay the cost.

Unmanageable debt can build up to the point that you owe more money than you can afford to pay back. When people get into debt, they can sometimes feel like they're trapped or that there is no way out.

Unmanageable debt can become a cycle that feels difficult to break. The cycle often looks like this:

PREDATORY LENDING

Even though there are many trusted lenders out there, like banks, it is important to be aware of another group of lenders, known as predatory lenders. These are institutions that lend money almost exclusively to people with low credit scores and a poor or non-existent credit history who struggle to get lines of credit from banks and other lenders.

A common form of predatory lending is a **payday loan.** This is a loan designed to give you an injection of cash to cover your bills and expenses until payday comes. The idea is that, once payday has arrived a week or two later, you will be able to pay that loan back with your wages. In reality, that is often not the case. These payday loans can have ridiculously high interest rates (ranging from 200% to over 1,000%). That means, when the borrower comes to repay the loan, it can cost hundreds of pounds more than what they initially borrowed, making it nearly impossible to pay back in one go.

With compound interest, this amount can keep climbing, leaving borrowers feeling as though they're stuck with this debt.

Many of these lenders aren't regulated and will sometimes deploy scare tactics such as sending people known as bailiffs to a borrower's home demanding to take their belongings to repay the debt.

It can be easy to fall into the trap of payday loans. Many websites that offer them use clever marketing – one showed me the exact time that I could have the money in my account (30 minutes from when I landed on the webpage) if I began an application straight away.

To avoid falling into this debt trap, it is best to steer clear of this type of loan and to only borrow from trusted sources such as a bank. On top of this, make sure that you only borrow what you will be able to repay and make a repayment plan to give you more peace of mind.

NEGATIVE IMPACT OF DEBT

Debt can have a negative impact, not just on your finances but also on your mental health. It can make you feel stressed, anxious or even depressed if you don't tackle it. That is why it's important to talk about how you're feeling with someone you trust and ask for help when you need it.

If you find yourself in debt, there are charities in the UK that are free and dedicated to giving you advice and support, such as:

 ★ STEPCHANGE

 ★ CITIZENS ADVICE

 ★ NATIONAL DEBTLINE

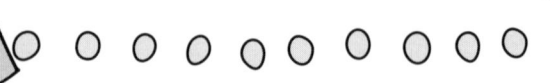

✓ What credit is, different types of credit and how compound interest works

✓ What credit history is and how credit scores are checked

✓ The difference between manageable and unmanageable debt

ACTION POINT

Want to put what you've learned into action?
Here's an activity to try.

In this chapter, we've discussed how credit works
and how it can impact your financial future.
It's time for you to take charge and begin the
journey of looking after your own credit history.

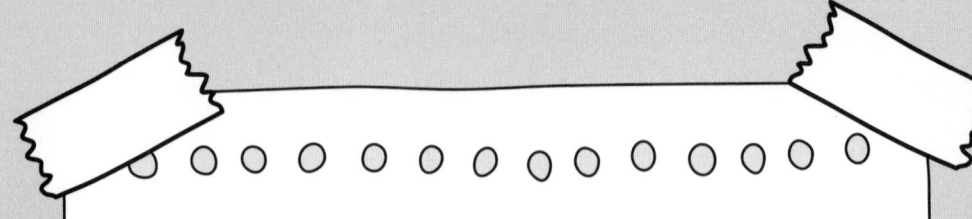

CHECK YOUR CREDIT SCORE

You'll only be able to check your credit score once you're over 18 because you're not able to apply for any lines of credit when you are younger than that and so you won't have a credit file. But, if you're 18 or over, you'll be able to check your credit score for free on any of the following platforms, which use data from the credit reference agencies mentioned earlier:

- ☑ EXPERIAN
- ☑ CLEARSCORE
- ☑ CREDIT KARMA
- ☑ EQUIFAX

Once you've signed up, you may find that you have a low/no credit score. This isn't something to panic about because it's likely you haven't got any lines of credit in your name yet.

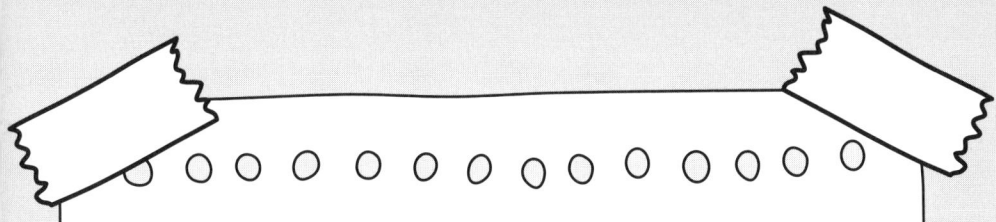

What you can do though is begin to take steps to build your credit score. Choose one of the following to give your credit score a boost:

★ Check that all of your personal details are correct on your credit reference agency profile (name, address, earnings, etc.).

★ Register to vote - aka join the electoral roll (you can do this from age 16 in England and Northern Ireland, and from 14 in Scotland and Wales).

★ Apply for a form of credit (do this responsibly).

★ Pay your bills on time (this includes phone bills).

The earlier that you take care of your credit score, the better the position you'll be in when you come to need it in the future.

4 KEEPING YOUR MONEY SAFE

FRAUD

TIME TO GET SECURE

So far in this book, you've learned how to
look after your money and what could happen
to your finances if you don't. But what happens
when things go wrong that are not your fault?
When you suddenly owe hundreds of pounds
on your credit card that you didn't spend?
There are people in the world who look to earn
money by pretending to be someone that they're
not. This is known as **fraud**.

WHAT IS FRAUD?

Fraud is when someone gains either money or
property through lying or tricking their victim.
Fraud is a criminal offence and is taken very
seriously in the UK. With the rise of social
media, these criminals have even more
chances to trick people out of their money.

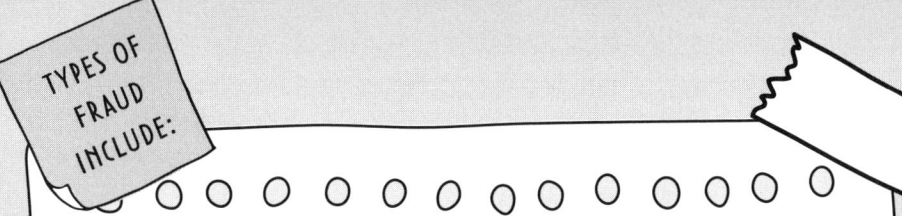

 **PRETENDING TO BE SOMEONE FROM A BANK VIA PHONE, EMAIL OR TEXT MESSAGE**

Someone pretending to be your bank might ask for your personal details (for example your name, address or PIN) or tell you to transfer money 'to keep it safe'. They may claim that your account has been compromised so your funds need to be moved, but in reality the other account is a fake that they have set up.

 **PRETENDING TO BE A FRIEND OR FAMILY MEMBER**

Criminals can impersonate the identities of friends or family members by cloning their phone numbers or email addresses, a type of **spoofing**. They might then ask for money or financial help and, because you believe it's the person that you know, you may fall into the trap of sending money.

 **A FAKE SOCIAL MEDIA COMPETITION**

Often, criminals will advertise competitions with extravagant prizes to entice you to click on a link and fill out your personal details, which they can then use to impersonate you online and steal money.

Criminals might attempt to get personal information from you, such as:

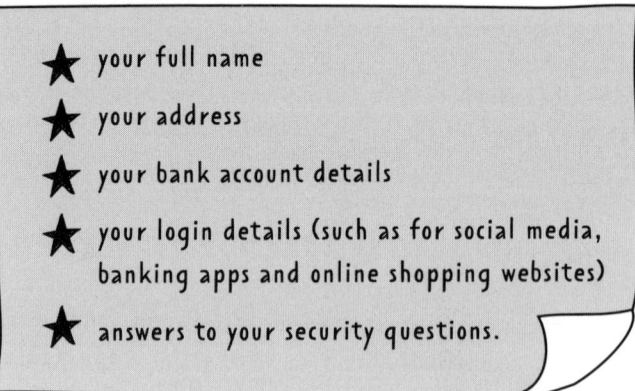

★ your full name

★ your address

★ your bank account details

★ your login details (such as for social media, banking apps and online shopping websites)

★ answers to your security questions.

Once they have this information, they can impersonate you online or, worse yet, try to steal money from you either directly from your bank account or through loans taken out in your name. This type of fraud is known as identity theft.

SPOTTING SCAMS

With people spending increasingly more time online, scammers have become more sophisticated with how they target their victims. In 2023, UK Finance reported that just under half of 18-24-year-olds have been contacted by a scammer pretending to be someone else. Of that group, over half have given money or personal details away. What this data shows is that young people, like yourself, are becoming targets of scammers and can be tricked into handing over personal details.

As well as the common examples discussed above, there are a few sophisticated scams that you need to be aware of.

MONEY MULES

A money mule is someone who allows other people to use their bank account to move or hold money, and they are often allowed to keep a small percentage as payment. A lot of people who become money mules are unaware of what they're getting themselves into.

SCAMS

The request may come from a trusted person such as a friend or loved one, or from criminals who target people with financial problems and pitch it as an 'easy way to make money'.

It's important to highlight that this is a form of **money laundering.** Money laundering is the movement of money that has come from illegal means (such as drug trafficking or fraud) and attempting to disguise where the money originally came from. One way to 'clean' this type of money is through other people's bank accounts.

REFUND SCAMS

This is when you're contacted and told that you're due a refund from a company or service. In the UK, scammers may pretend to be **HMRC (His Majesty's Revenue and Customs),** telling you that you're due a refund on your tax return (a form declaring how much income and assets someone has so tax can be calculated). The goal of this scam is to get potential victims to share personal details such as banking information, and sometimes money, with the false promise that you will receive a refund into your account.

'GET RICH QUICK' SCAMS

This is when someone approaches you with a great 'business opportunity' that promises to pay much more than what you initially invest. The potential victim is sold a dream that a company or product they invest in will generate a lot of money in a short space of time, making it a way to 'get rich quick'. The goal of this scam is to steal the 'investment' money from victims, as well as their personal details in some cases.

TIPS FOR SPOTTING SCAMS

It can be difficult at times to figure out what is a scam and what isn't, as they're not all as obvious as you might think. To protect yourself from potential scammers, here are a few tips that you should go through before parting with any cash or personal details.

If in doubt, talk to someone you trust. If someone approaches you with an opportunity that makes you feel uncomfortable, talk to a friend or family member and voice your concern. It can also be useful to share the information with your bank so they can be aware of potential scams and give you tips to protect yourself.

Who does the message claim to be from? Do you have an account with that company? Check that the actual phone number or email address matches the company details available online, or for family and friends, check that it matches the one you have saved in your contacts.

+44 7123 456789
Today, 21:09

Halifax: Check out our new savings account with the best interest rats just for you. Limited avaibility only. Visit https://Halifax.OurNew-Account.net to start TODAY.

Check the grammar and spelling of the message, and the style it is written in. Is that how you would expect the person to write?

Ask yourself, does this opportunity seem too good to be true? If the answer is yes, it probably is. If it was that easy to make money then everyone would be doing it! Who will really benefit from the transaction?

When was the message sent? Does your mum normally email you in the middle of the night? Most companies will also send communications during business hours.

Is the message pressuring you to do something urgently with little explanation? Take a step back and assess how urgent it really is. If it's warning about an issue with an account, log in to the account separately to check if something is actually wrong.

New Email
From: mum@google123.com
To: an.other@yahoo.co.uk
Subject: Help, need money!!!
Sent: Yesterday, 03:21

Hi! It's mum here.
I'm in an emergency. It's really urgent.
I've been locked out of my account and need money to pay the bills quickly.
Please can you send me £200 NOW!
http://western-uni.on/transferME.
Thank you!

Don't click on any links you receive in suspicious emails or messages. Some links can lead you to fake websites that will attempt to steal personal information or put a virus on your computer.

101

HOW TO STAY SAFE ONLINE

You've just seen the various ways that scammers may attempt to steal money and details from you, but no need to panic! It might sound scary, but there are things that you can do to protect your accounts from scammers looking for quick cash.

CREATE STRONG PASSWORDS

For any kind of digital account (for example banking, social media or online shopping), make sure that you choose a strong password. Don't choose words and numbers that are personal to you, such as your birthday, your address, your family's names or your pet's name. Instead, choose three random words, a number and two special characters – like 'AppleWindowBoots3!&'. This makes your password easy to remember but harder to crack. Alternatively, you could use an online random password generator to create a strong password.

Password
(**)
///////////
weak

Password
(****)
/////////////////
medium

Password
(******)
///////////////////////
strong

KEEP YOUR PASSWORDS SAFE

Make sure not to repeat the same password for each new site you sign up to. Repeating your password leaves your details vulnerable to scammers who may have been able to find your password from breaching the security of a different website. It's also crucial to never share your password with anyone, even your loved ones.

USE TWO-FACTOR AUTHENTICATION

This is an additional layer of protection on your accounts that requires two different forms of identification. Most social media accounts have this option, which you're able to turn on in the settings, and banking apps tend to have this by default. The first step is to log in with your password as normal. The second step works by either sending a code to your mobile phone or using a separate app that generates a code to confirm that it is you signing in. To protect you even further, these codes expire every 30 seconds, making it very difficult for someone to copy the code and attempt to log in as you. Think of it as having two front doors that require separate keys to open before you're able to get into your house.

DON'T SAVE YOUR BANK CARDS ON WEBSITES

Online retailers will often give you the option to save your card details when you reach the checkout to make paying faster in the future. The problem is that many websites do not have the correct level of security to keep your details safe. It's not just individuals who can be victims of cybercrime – so can businesses. Sometimes, scammers will target businesses to steal customer information or funds. Instead of saving your card details, input your payment details each time that you pay for any item online, or use Apply Pay or Google Pay for a secure time-saving option.

USE SECURE PAYMENT METHODS

As you learned in Chapter 2, purchases made on a credit card are protected by Section 75 of the Consumer Credit Act, and purchases made using a debit card may be covered by the chargeback scheme. If you're making a purchase on a website that you can't confirm is secure or that you haven't used before, it may be wise to use a credit card to complete the transaction, so you have an added layer of security.

WHAT TO DO IF YOU THINK YOU'VE BEEN A VICTIM OF A SCAM OR FRAUD

Get in contact with your bank as soon as you know your account has been breached and/or funds have been transferred out of your account. Supply your bank with as much information as you can regarding the scam and how it took place so they can give you useful next steps.

If you're worried, turn to someone that you trust. This could be a parent, family member or family friend. Whoever you choose, it's better to share what has happened than keep it to yourself.

✓ What fraud is

✓ The different types of scams and how to spot them

✓ How to protect your personal information and your money online

✓ What to do if you think you've been a victim of a scam or fraud

ACTION POINT

Want to put what you've learned into action? Here's an activity to try.

You've learned about different scams and ways to keep yourself safe online, so let's put your knowledge to the test!

Follow the instructions over the page to practise identifying scams and see how many red flags you can spot.

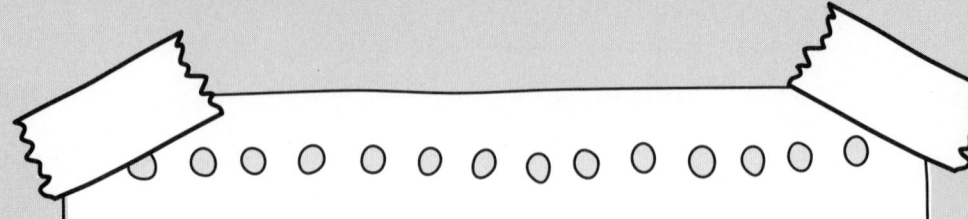

SPOT THE SCAM

1. Identify the scam – first, research to find examples of online scams and frauds that have recently been reported in the news. Check a range of news websites, online security blogs and TV shows to see what's current.

2. Find the red flags – for each example, find the red flags that suggest that this is a scam. These could include:

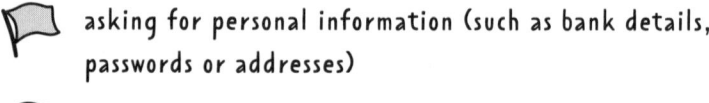 asking for personal information (such as bank details, passwords or addresses)

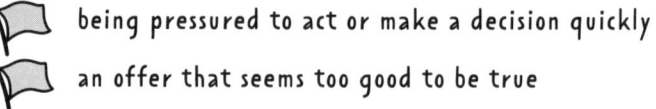 being pressured to act or make a decision quickly

an offer that seems too good to be true

incorrect grammar or spelling

 website links or email addresses that look suspicious.

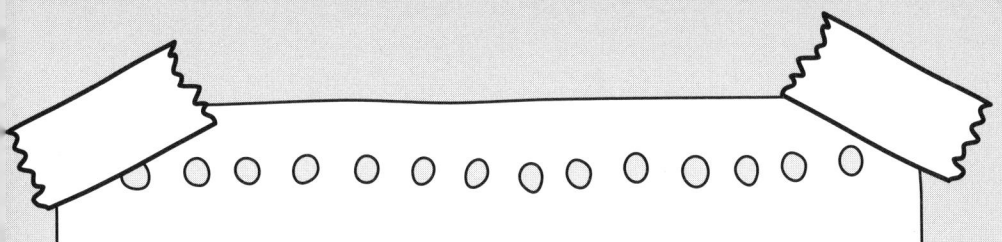

3. Practise online safety – now you know what to look out for, take this time to review your security settings for your online accounts:

☑ Choose an account (email, social media, online shopping).

☑ Review your password and update it to a strong password with a unique combination of letters, numbers and special characters.

☑ If available, enable two-factor authentication on your account and make sure that your contact information is up to date.

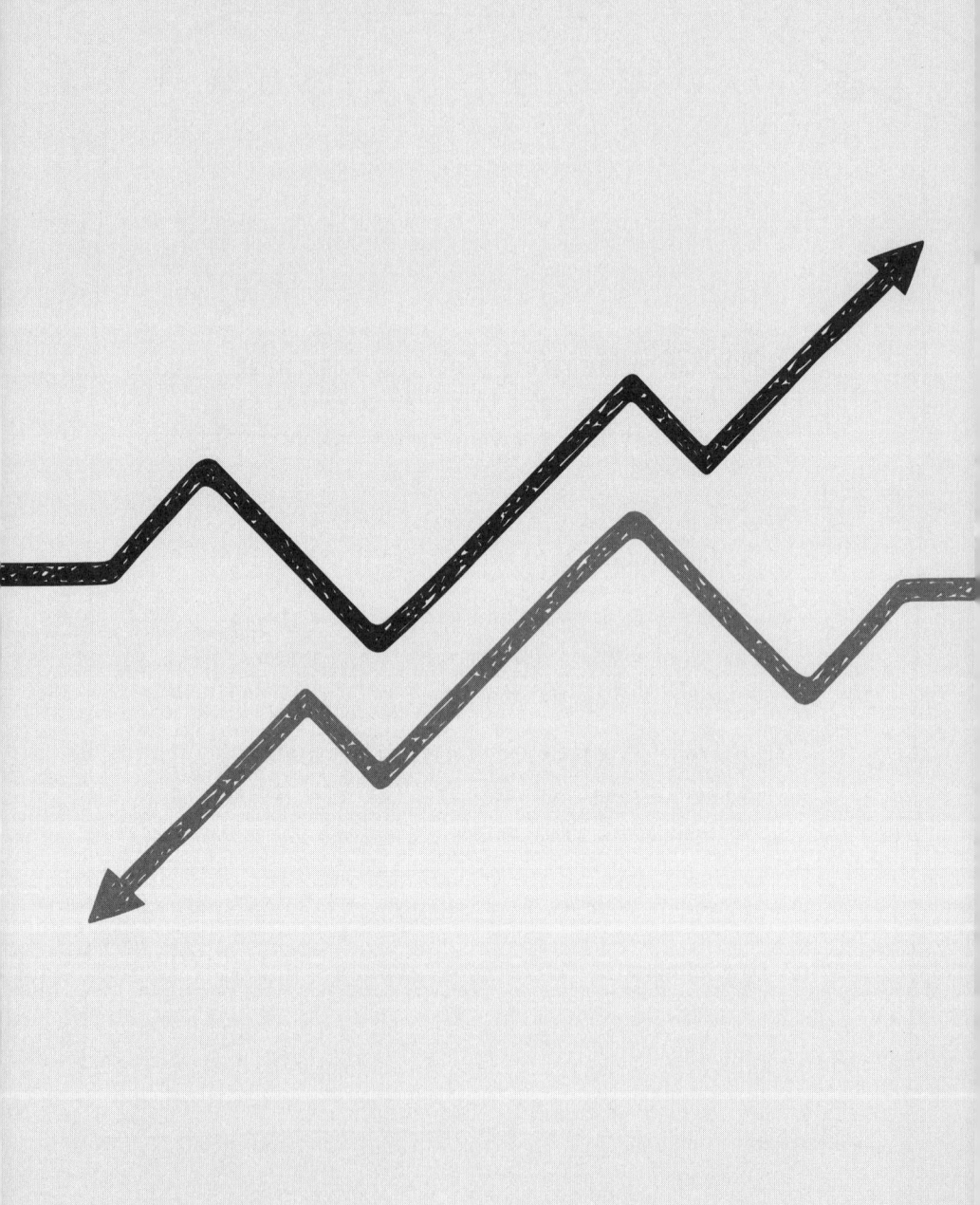

5 INTRO TO INVESTING & RISK

INVESTING

When you hear the word **investing**, what's the first thing that comes to mind? That it's something only rich people can afford to do? Those people who sit in front of computers all day frantically buying and selling these mysterious things called stocks? What if I told you that you don't need to have millions in the bank to get started? That you can grow your money with very little work? Sounds interesting, doesn't it?

WHAT EXACTLY IS INVESTING?

Investing is the process of buying **assets** with the hope that they will increase in value over time and earn you a profit. An asset is something of value that you can sell for money. An example could be a property, a car or even collector's items such as stamps or handbags.

Let's say that you manage to get your hands on a rare set of trading cards. You buy the set for **£5** and decide to keep it somewhere safe, unopened. After a year, you decide to sell it online to potential collectors. Over that past year, the card set has become increasingly difficult to find, causing its value to increase. An interested buyer offers you **£50** for your set of cards, making you a profit of **£45**. This is how investing works.

Investing involves putting money away for the long term, hoping that you can get back more money than you originally put in. There are many reasons why you might want to begin investing – to buy a house, to be able to afford your dream holiday, to save for retirement. The list is endless. But, before you can start investing money, you'll need to understand how it works and what you're able to invest in.

WHAT CAN I INVEST IN?

You could invest by buying a business, a property or even rare assets such as art or jewellery. However, you can also buy **shares** and invest in the **stock market**.

The stock market (also sometimes called the stock exchange) is the place where investors buy and sell shares of a company. In the UK, the main stock markets are the FTSE 100 and the London Stock Exchange. On these stock markets, there is a list of **publicly traded companies** selling shares that investors can buy. Put simply, a publicly traded company is a company that is listed on the stock market and sells shares of its company to the public. The opposite of this is privately held companies that are under private ownership. They may issue shares to individuals, but they are not listed on the stock market and do not sell shares to the public.

WHAT IS A SHARE?

A share is part-ownership of a company. Let's imagine you buy a share in my company, Pennies to Pounds. That means you now own

114

a part of Pennies to Pounds, and that makes you a **shareholder**. Companies sell a lot of shares, sometimes in the thousands. Depending on how many shares in a company you have, you might be given a say in how the business is run by attending shareholder meetings. Some companies also pay **dividends** (rewards that are paid to shareholders when companies make a profit as a thank you for investing). You might buy shares because, when the company does well, the value of it (and therefore of your shares) goes up. This means that when you go to sell your shares, you will get back more than you originally paid for them, making a profit However, it's important to remember that your investments could also fall in value if the company doesn't do as well. If this happens, you will get back less than you initially paid for the shares.

OTHER INVESTMENTS

There are also other assets that you can invest your money in.

A **bond** is an asset that is sold by companies and governments to raise money. The best way to

explain it is like an IOU. Imagine the government is selling £5 bonds. If you buy one of the bonds, you have essentially given the government £5 to borrow. Bonds have something called a term, which is how long the company plans to borrow the money for. There's also an interest rate on a bond, which is how much the company will repay you at the end of the term, on top of what has been borrowed. So, let's say the government bond has a three-year term with a 2% interest rate. After the three years, the government gives you back your initial investment of £5 as well as an extra 10p (2% interest) as a thank you for buying the bond.

An **ETF (exchange-traded fund)** is a collection of different types of investments. An ETF could include a range of shares, bonds and other assets. The only difference is, they are sold on the stock market, just like shares. So, you could purchase one ETF like you would one share, but you would have a range of different investments within it.

NOTE: Investing means that your money is at risk. Your investments can go up as well as down. If you're unsure, make sure to ask for the help of a professional.

Investment products in the UK are regulated by the Prudential Regulation Authority. Regulation gives you peace of mind to know that banks and investment companies are legitimate and it offers you a level of protection for your money.

COMPOUND INTEREST

This is one of the amazing wonders when it comes to saving and investing. As discussed in Chapter 3, compound interest is interest on top of interest – but it can apply to interest you earn as well as what you owe! Let's break it down:

Imagine you have invested **£100** and earn **5%** interest on your money. At the end of the year, you will have **£105**. If you leave that money saved/invested, in year two you will now earn **5%** interest on **£105**. At the end of year two, you will have **£110.25**. If you continue to save/invest that money, in year three you will now earn **5%** interest on **£110.25**. At the end of year three, you will have **£115.76**. This cycle continues the longer you leave your money in savings/investments, allowing your money to grow even more.

RISK

HOW DO I CHOOSE WHAT TO INVEST IN?

To decide what to invest in, it's important to understand your **risk appetite**. A risk appetite (or attitude to risk) is how cautious you are looking to be with your investments. Once you know your risk appetite, you can decide which investment product(s) are right for you.

A good way to decide your risk appetite is to first understand your goals for your money. For example, if in the next five years you want to use your investment money to buy a house, you will want to be confident that you're going to get back what you put in. This might mean that you have a low risk appetite. On the flip side, if your goal is to save money to travel the world in ten years' time, you might be willing to take more risk with your investments in the hope that you get back a lot more than you put in. This might mean that you have a high risk appetite.

Let's put this into context by looking at the risk associated with each of the investment products we've learned about so far.

★ Shares are typically seen as higher-risk investment products, as how much you get back depends on how well the company does. If the company has a bad year or, worse yet, goes bust or **bankrupt**, there is a high chance that you will get back much less than you initially invested.

★ ETFs are seen as medium-risk investment products because they contain a mix of different investment types, spreading out the risk.

★ Bonds are typically seen as lower-risk investment products as they are usually given out by governments, who are seen to be safer and more reliable.

LOW   HIGH

WHERE CAN YOU INVEST?

There are many different platforms that allow you to begin investing in the stock market with as little as £1. However, rather than buying and selling individual shares yourself, you can also choose to let a bank make those decisions (and take on some of the risk) for you.

You learned about stocks and shares ISAs, junior stocks and shares ISAs, and stocks and shares LISAs in Chapter 1. These are accounts where the money that you've saved is invested into other companies through the stock market. This is done through investing your money in something called an investment fund – a group of different companies that are put together under one fund and managed by a fund manager. You can't choose what companies are within each fund but you can choose the type of fund that you invest in. For example, you could choose a tech fund (investing in companies that are in the tech industry, such as Apple and Microsoft) or an environmental fund.

DID YOU KNOW?

Ethical investing is when you put your money into investment products that don't compromise your morals and beliefs. It's important to research where your money is being invested. Some investment funds may be investing your money into companies that produce oil, coal and metals which are harmful for the environment. There are platforms that allow you to invest your money into 'ethical funds' (funds that don't contain companies that negatively impact the environment or society), however you can also do this yourself by looking at the funds that your money is invested in and switching to a more ethical fund.

SHARIA-COMPLIANT INVESTMENT FUNDS

If you're a practising Muslim, you may not be able to invest in some of the products mentioned above. There are investment funds available that are Sharia-compliant, meaning they follow the requirements of Sharia law and the principles of Islam. These funds are also considered a type of ethical investing.

Sharia-compliant funds must follow several rules. These include not investing in gambling, alcohol or tobacco, and donating non-compliant income, like interest, to charity.

There are a small number of investment platforms that offer Sharia-compliant investment funds so be sure to do your research to find one that suits you.

OTHER TYPES OF SAVING

As mentioned earlier, investing your money is a way to help your money grow over the long term. However, if you have a low risk appetite, savings accounts can be a good starting point. We discussed the different accounts where you can save money in Chapter 1, and it can be worth splitting your savings between a few of these to take advantage of the different advantages they offer.

CRYPTOCURRENCY

There is a growing interest in other forms of investment, namely digital investments. The most popular that you've likely heard of is **cryptocurrency**. Cryptocurrency is a type of digital currency that can be used as a form of payment. Unlike regular currency, cryptocurrency is **decentralised**, meaning that there is no central bank to manage its value like the Bank of England in the UK. Because of how the computer code is written, payments using cryptocurrencies are anonymous and this type of currency cannot be faked. The decentralisation makes cryptocurrencies a lot more volatile than other currencies (and other investment products such as stocks and shares), meaning the value of it can rise and fall very quickly.

There are thousands of different cryptocurrencies but the one that is talked about the most is **bitcoin.** Bitcoin can be used like government-issued money (known as **fiat currency**) to purchase items and services online. However, many people purchase bitcoin as a way to make more money. Like the investment

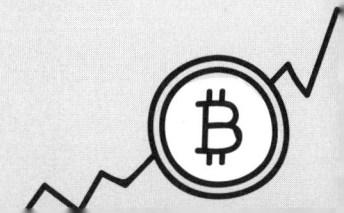

products discussed earlier in this chapter, cryptocurrency is also sold on exchanges (a place where investors are able to buy, sell or trade cryptocurrency). This makes it another type of investment, as the value of different cryptocurrencies can go up and down just like shares and ETFs.

Even though it's another type of investment, cryptocurrencies are not regulated in the UK as of April 2024. This means that what you buy or sell when it comes to cryptocurrencies isn't monitored, making you a potential target of dodgy schemes or platforms. Despite how it is sometimes shown online, cryptocurrency isn't an easy way to 'get rich quick' (remember that from Chapter 4?). As with any investment, there is risk. You may see stories of people making thousands from cryptocurrency, but there are plenty more stories of people who have lost their entire life savings. Make sure you've done your research before making any investments into a cryptocurrency.

FINFLUENCERS AND FINANCIAL EDUCATORS

As someone who has been creating content around financial education for a few years now, I'm seen as a 'finfluencer'. A finfluencer is just as it sounds – an influencer who is in the financial  space. There weren't very many people making content about money when I first started. Now it seems that with every other swipe, a new person is trying to tell you how to spend your money and what to invest in.

You don't need a qualification to create content on money and finance, plus there is no official way to verify who is a source to trust for online content. If you're seeking financial advice, the FCA (Financial Conduct Authority) has a register of qualified financial advisors that you can speak with. When it comes to social media content, some creators spread incorrect information and disguise it as fact. Before  listening to any 'advice' online, make sure that you do your research on who is sharing the information and whether they can be trusted.

GAMBLING

As you've learned in this chapter so far, investing is a way to grow your money and hopefully get back more than you initially put in. But sometimes that desire for 'fast money' and 'quick returns' can lead people down a dangerous route – **gambling**.

Gambling is when you bet (or risk) money or other valuables on a game of chance that you can't control. Imagine you're playing a card game. You bet £5 that the next card in the deck is going to be the Queen of Hearts, with your opponent promising to pay you £10 if you're right. The card is revealed and it's not the card that you bet on, so you lose £5. You decide to try again to see if you can 'win back' the money that you lost and get it wrong again, losing a total of £10.

This can become an out-of-control habit. Many people become addicted to the feeling of winning and will continue to bet money, even if they lose, to chase that win again. Sometimes people can find themselves gambling more than they can afford and they end up in debt as a result.

If you ever find yourself struggling with a gambling addiction or know someone who is, here are some things that you can do:

- ☑ Confide in someone that you trust who you know won't judge you. This could be a friend, family member or professional.

- ☑ Avoid going to gambling centres, such as casinos or bingo halls, so you reduce the temptation to take part.

- ☑ Try to find a new hobby or activity that you can take part in to fill the gap of gambling.

There are organisations in the UK that you can turn to if you need professional help, such as:

★ **GAMCARE**

★ **SAMARITANS**

★ **GAMBLING AWARE**

✓ What investing is

✓ The types of product you can invest in

✓ What cryptocurrency is

✓ What 'finfluencers' are

✓ What gambling is and how to seek help if you need it

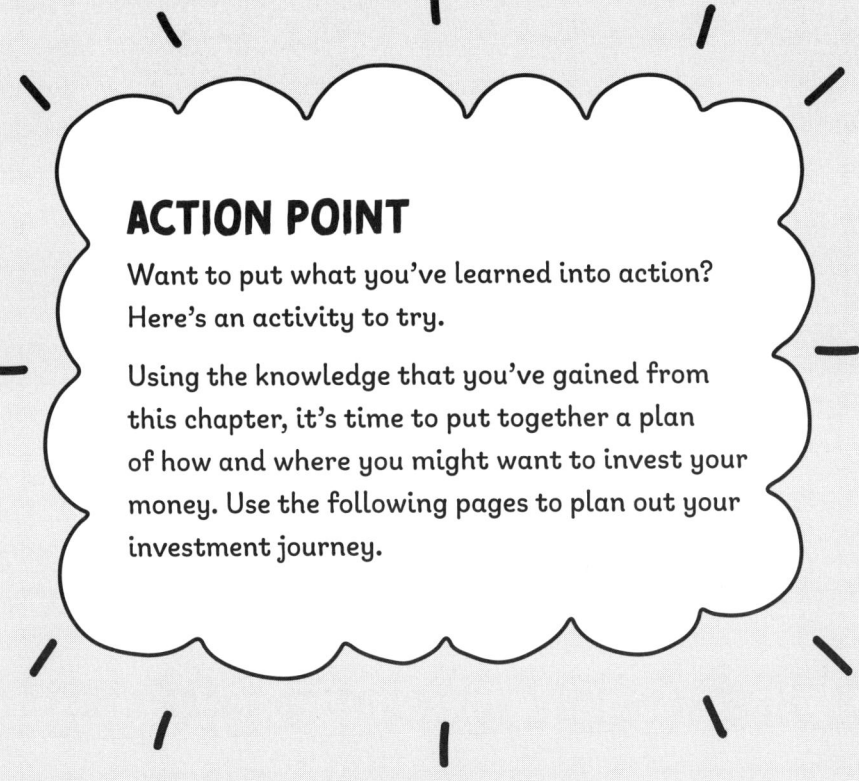

ACTION POINT

Want to put what you've learned into action?
Here's an activity to try.

Using the knowledge that you've gained from
this chapter, it's time to put together a plan
of how and where you might want to invest your
money. Use the following pages to plan out your
investment journey.

CREATE YOUR OWN INVESTMENT PLAN

This plan will give you an understanding of what you want
to do with your money when it comes to investing.

What is your goal?

(for instance buying a new phone or going on a trip abroad)

‐ ‐

‐ ‐

How much money do you want to save/invest?

‐ ‐

‐ ‐

How often do you want to save/invest?

(monthly, quarterly or yearly)

‐ ‐

‐ ‐

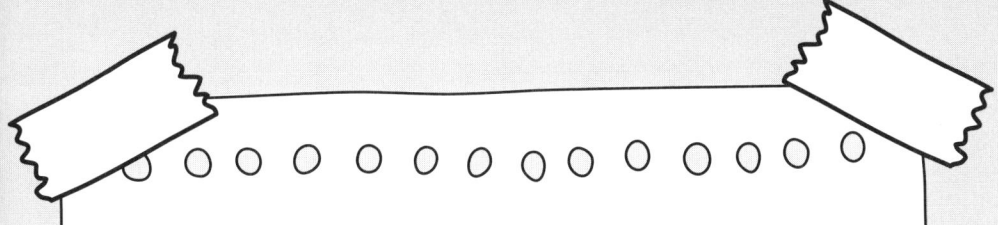

What investment option(s) do you want to try?

(junior ISA, stocks and shares ISA, etc.)

How long do you want to keep your money invested for?

6 PLANNING FOR THE FUTURE

STUDENT FINANCE

SO WHAT'S NEXT?

Whether you head off to university, go down the apprenticeship route or jump straight into the world of work, once you're officially done with school you'll be diving headfirst into the world of adulting. This is an exciting time, as your life can become anything you want it to be. Whatever you choose to do next, money will be at the centre of it. In this chapter, you'll learn how payslips and taxes work, as well as ways to financially plan for your future.

PAYING FOR UNI

For a lot of teenagers, the next step after school and college is to attend university. Those of you that choose to go down this route will likely have to pay for your tuition costs with a **student loan.** The way you apply for the loan, the amount on offer and the terms of repayment vary across the UK. Wherever you live, though, it is the government that provides the money. If you're still in education, your school or college will help you apply.

☑ In England, the Student Loans Company administers loans, which you must apply for via Student Finance England.

☑ In Scotland, the Student Awards Agency Scotland (SAAS) is the company that issues loans and bursaries to students.

☑ In Wales, Student Finance Wales is the company that issues loans and grants to students.

☑ In Northern Ireland, Student Finance Northern Ireland is the company that issues loans, grants and allowances to students.

The application process for student finance consists of two components:

☑ your details (for example where you live, what you're going to study and where you're looking to study)

☑ your parents' or guardians' details (for example what they do for work and how much they earn).

A tuition fee loan covers the full cost of your course, and is not means-tested. If you need an additional loan to help pay for rent and other living costs while at university, this is called a **maintenance loan.**

If you do not make an application with your parents' or guardians' details, or they earn over a certain amount, you may only be entitled to the minimum student loan amount of £3,790. If you're from a low-income household or you have an estranged parent or parents (i.e. you're applying as an individual because you don't live with your parents), you could be entitled to the maximum student loan amount of £13,348 (or £10,227 if you are studying outside London). Depending on how much your parents or guardians earn, the student loan amount granted to you could also vary within the minimum and maximum amount. (These figures are correct for 2024/25.)

You need to reapply for a student loan for each year that you're studying at university, and most students will only receive cover for four years of study (unless the course that you are studying is longer than that, such as medicine or dentistry).

Let's fast forward to the end of your university course – congratulations, you've graduated! Now it's time to start thinking about repaying your tuition and/or maintenance loan. No need to stress about finding the cash straight away! You only begin making repayments on your student loan in the April after you've graduated and once you earn over a certain threshold.

The amount that you repay depends on what plan you're on, and you can find more details about that through your account and the government website. Once you start repaying your student loan, the payments will be taken out of your wages automatically and will show up under the 'deductions' section of your payslip (see pages 140-141).

STUDENT BANK ACCOUNTS

When you're heading to university, you'll be eligible to open a student bank account. These accounts are just like normal current accounts that we covered in Chapter 1 but they have a number of perks specifically for students:

0% interest overdraft – the biggest benefit of these accounts for students is the fee-free overdraft. You're able to borrow money from this account and pay no interest on what's borrowed for the agreed period of time. This is usually for the period of your study but some accounts may require you to bring the overdraft balance back to zero before you progress to your next year of study. The amount that you're able to borrow depends on the account provider but some banks allow you to borrow up to £3,000 interest-free.

Discount cards and cashback – some providers offer additional perks to students such as a free 4-year railcard to purchase train tickets throughout the UK at a reduced rate, or a 4-year Tastecard for discounts at restaurants and coffee shops. You may also be able to get cashback at certain retailers depending on the account that you choose.

Even though the biggest benefit of a student bank account is the 0% interest overdraft, it is important to remember that this is a form of borrowing so you need to ensure that you have a plan to pay this money back. Many accounts change into 'graduate accounts' once you graduate from university and may require you to bring the balance back to zero within a specific time frame or they may begin to charge interest on the money borrowed.

PAYSLIPS

UNDERSTANDING YOUR PAYSLIP

When you begin working your first job, whether it's a part-time job or an entry-level position, on your first payday you will receive something called a **payslip**. A payslip is a note that breaks down how much you're being paid and how much of your pay is being **deducted** for taxes and insurance. There are a few key aspects of your payslip that are important to understand:

National Insurance
– this is how much of your pay is taken out towards your National Insurance contributions.

Student Loan
– if you attended university in the UK and took out a student loan, this is how much is taken out to repay your loan.

Pension
– this is how much of your pay is taken out and contributed towards your retirement pot.

Tax Code
- this is the code that each employee is given so employers know how much tax each worker needs to pay. It is made up of a combination of numbers and a letter.

PAYE Tax
- this stands for 'pay as you earn' and it is how income tax (the tax that you pay on the money you've earned) and National Insurance are deducted.

Employee Number	Employee Name	Process Date	National Insurance Number	
87021	Ms A N Other	28/05/24	AB 12 34 56 C	
Payments	**Units**	**Rate**	**Amount**	**Deductions**	
Basic Salary			1335.92	PAYE Tax	71.26
Overtime	5.5	12.36	67.98	Nat. Insurance	28.47
				Pension	70.19
				Student Loan	0
		Total Payments	1403.90	Total	169.92
				Year to Date	
Tax Code	1000L			Pay to Date	2807.80
Tax Period	6			Tax to Date	142.52
Method	BACS			NI to Date	56.94
				Taxable to Date	2807.80
				Net Pay	1233.98

Total Payments
- also known as Gross Pay, this number shows how much you're going to get paid before deductions are made.

Net Pay
- this number (also known as your take-home pay), typically at the bottom of your payslip, shows how much you're going to be paid after all the deductions have been made.

WHAT IS INCOME TAX?

Income tax is a percentage of your income that you must pay regularly to the government. In the UK, income tax is used to fund public services such as the NHS and schools, as well as to invest in public projects such as fixing roads and constructing housing.

The way that your income is taxed depends on how much you earn and what band that money falls into. Your income is separated into the basic, higher and additional income tax band rates. Every worker is entitled to something called a **personal allowance**, which is the amount of money you can earn without paying any tax. This book is being written during the tax year 2024/2025, and the personal allowance rate is frozen until April 2028, so for the next few years it is:

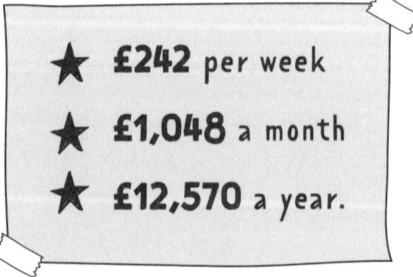

★ **£242** per week

★ **£1,048** a month

★ **£12,570** a year.

Any money that you earn over that amount is taxed at different rates, which at the time of writing look like this:

BASIC RATE: 20% tax charged on any income between **£12,571** and **£50,270**.

HIGHER RATE: 40% tax charged on any income between **£50,271** and **£125,140**.

ADDITIONAL RATE: 45% tax charged on any income over **£125,140**.

It's important to note that you don't pay the next band rate on all your income when you get a pay increase, only on every pound you earn above that threshold.

For example, let's say someone earns **£55,000** a year:

PERSONAL ALLOWANCE: £0 in tax up to £12,570

BASIC RATE: 20% tax for their earnings between £12,571 and £50,270, i.e. 20% of £37,699 = £7,539.80

HIGHER RATE: 40% tax for their earnings between £50,271 and £55,000, i.e. 40% of £4,729 = £1,891.60

TOTAL TAX: £9,431.40

The amount of income tax that you need to pay is shown in the form of your tax code. Your tax code is calculated like this:

> # The amount that you can earn before paying tax ÷ 10 + a letter added.

For example, if your personal allowance is £12,570 a year, your tax code might be 1257L.

Sometimes your tax code can be wrong, for example if you've recently moved to a new job or work more than one job. It's crucial to check your payslip as you could be paying too much in tax. If you're ever unsure, speak to the human resources or accounts team at your workplace or give HMRC a call to double-check. HMRC is in charge of collecting money that pays for the UK's public services and offers financial support to families and households in need.

WHAT IS NATIONAL INSURANCE?

National Insurance is a type of tax that helps to pay for government benefits (such as Jobseeker's Allowance) and the State Pension (more on that on page 147). Unlike income tax, you only pay National Insurance once you receive your **National Insurance number.** You'll automatically receive a letter through the post with your number three months before your 16th birthday.

For the tax year 2024/25, payments only begin once:

★ you're an employee earning more than **£242** a week, or

★ you're self-employed making a profit of more than **£12,570** a year.

PENSIONS

There are different classes that you may fall into depending on whether you're employed or self-employed. That can get a bit complicated but, if you're employed, you will fall under Class 1. At the time of writing, the National Insurance bands are:

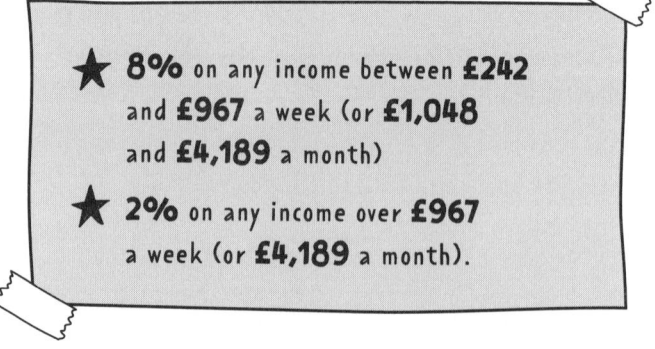

★ **8%** on any income between **£242** and **£967** a week (or **£1,048** and **£4,189** a month)

★ **2%** on any income over **£967** a week (or **£4,189** a month).

We've covered a lot of numbers when it comes to income tax and National Insurance, but you don't need to be a maths whizz to understand this! This breakdown is to help you understand how these deductions are calculated. All the above calculations are done for you by your employer, so you don't need to worry about that – all you need to do is check your payslip regularly to make sure that your codes and deductions are correct.

WHAT IS A PENSION?

When you hear the word 'retirement', what comes to mind? If I had to guess, I reckon you'd say something along the lines of 'old people' Even though you are many years away from retirement, it's extremely important to start thinking about it as early as possible.

A pension is a pot that you save into that will be used to fund your lifestyle when you come to retire (i.e. stop working). In the UK, everyone who has contributed to their National Insurance for enough years is entitled to something called the **State Pension.** As of 2024, the current State Pension amount is £221.20 a week and the age that you can claim that amount is from 66 years old.

Doesn't sound like a lot of money, does it? Well, that's because it isn't. Thankfully, there are other pension pots that you're able to use to top up your retirement fund.

WORKPLACE PENSION

Once you're employed, over the age of 22
and earn more than £10,000 per tax year,
your employer will automatically enrol you into
a **workplace pension.** This is a pension pot that
both you and your employer pay money into
each month. The minimum amount of money
that needs to be paid into your workplace
pension is 8% of your earnings, but that whole
amount doesn't have to just come from you. Your
employer must contribute a minimum of 3% to
your workplace pension, meaning that you would
only need to pay 5% of your income to make up
the 8% minimum.

Once income tax and National Insurance have
been deducted from your pay, an extra 5%
deduction into your workplace pension may seem
like it's not worth it as you could use that money
right now. However, what makes workplace
pensions such a great retirement pot is the
employer contributions. The way that I like to
look at these contributions is almost as if you're
getting a pay rise, but you'll be able to have that
extra cash when you stop working and retire.
Some employers may contribute more than the

minimum 3% or, better yet, match the percentage that you put into your pension pot. It's important to highlight that your employer will only keep making contributions as long as you do. The moment that you choose to opt out (stop paying money in), your employer will stop too.

There are many benefits to paying into your pension, but it's important to remember that you may experience different situations throughout your life when it comes to your money. There may come a time when costs rise, and your money doesn't buy as many things as it once did. You might decide to opt out of your pension so you can have a bit more money coming in each month. But, while only you can decide if and when you opt out, it's important to remember to opt back in and continue making pension contributions when you can afford to again.

OPT IN ☑

OPT OUT ☐

PERSONAL PENSION

If you are looking to put more money into your retirement savings or you're self-employed, you might look to open a **personal pension.** This is a pension pot that you can open yourself and make contributions to. There are several platforms online that allow you to set up a personal pension and it's a very simple process. Having both a workplace pension and a personal pension can allow you to grow your money for your retirement while also being able to control how much or little you'd like to contribute.

I could talk for days about the importance of pensions. But all you need to remember is, even though your retirement might seem years and years away, it's beneficial to start saving towards it as early as possible. Pension funds (including all work and personal pensions) are also a form of investment, as your money is invested into the stock market with the hope of getting back more money than you initially saved. The earlier that you start, the more you can have in your pot to spend your retirement relaxing and travelling the world (or whatever you choose to do at that age).

✓ How student finance works

✓ How to read a payslip

✓ What income tax and National Insurance are

✓ The importance of pensions

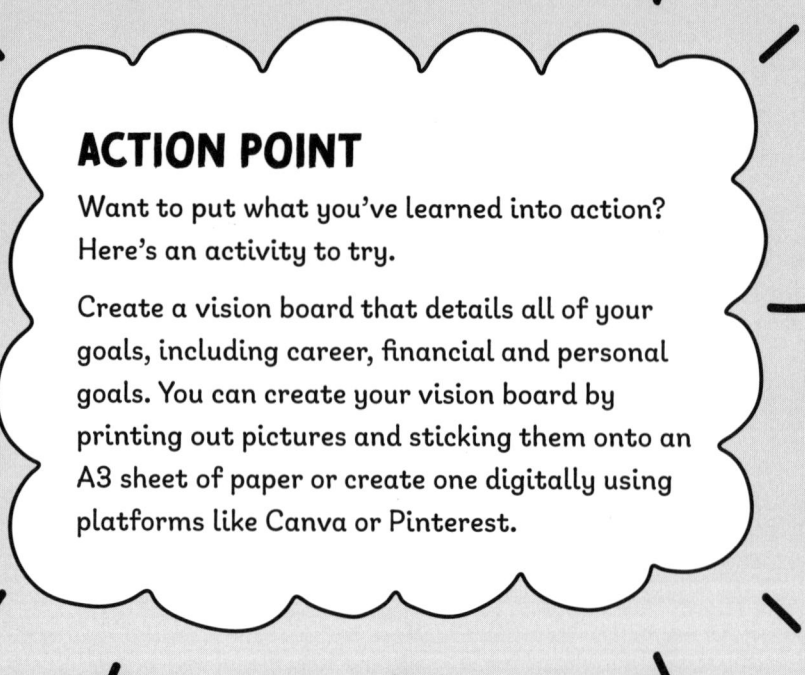

ACTION POINT

Want to put what you've learned into action?
Here's an activity to try.

Create a vision board that details all of your
goals, including career, financial and personal
goals. You can create your vision board by
printing out pictures and sticking them onto an
A3 sheet of paper or create one digitally using
platforms like Canva or Pinterest.

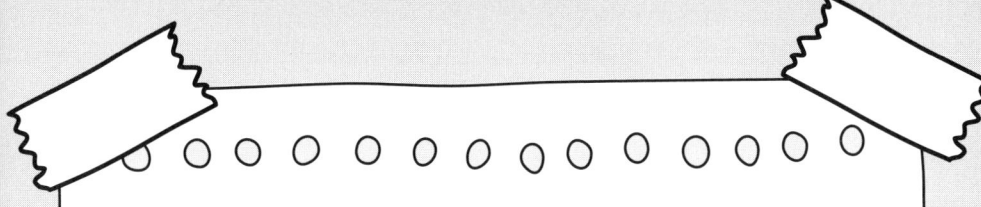

Create a vision board

Your vision board is there to keep you on track and motivated to reach your goals. You could include:

★ What you want to do when you finish school and how much it may cost you (university, apprenticeship or straight into work)

★ Your dream job/career

★ What your ideal retirement will look like (and how much you'll put into your pension)

★ What you're currently saving/investing towards

Make sure to keep the vision board somewhere that you can refer to it regularly – on your wall if you created it physically or as your phone/computer background if you created a digital vision board.

AND THAT'S IT,
WE'VE REACHED THE END!

We've been on quite the financial journey together, haven't we? From understanding the basics of budgeting to financially planning for your retirement.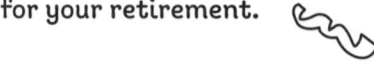

Let's take a minute to look back at what you've learned. You know that money isn't just something that you use to buy things – it's a tool that can help you to achieve your life goals. You've learned how to budget and save your money so it can stretch further, what investing is and how to use credit responsibly. You know how taxes work, ways to identify potential scams and why it's necessary to plan for your future.

The most important thing that you've gained though is confidence to take control of your finances. You've now got the knowledge and skills to build the future that you've envisioned.

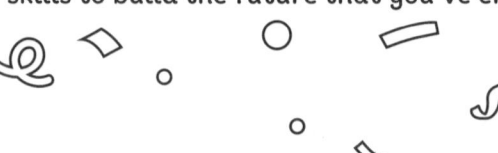

BUT YOUR FINANCIAL EDUCATION CONTINUES...

Even though this book has come to an end, continue to be curious about money – ask questions, listen to podcasts and watch videos and read articles online. Finance is always changing, with the government bringing in new rules and products all of the time. This is what makes the world of money an exciting one.

If you want to continue this momentum and keep learning, you can head over to the Pennies to Pounds website where you'll find plenty of articles, videos and resources to help you handle your money.

My final note to you is this: you are more than capable of achieving anything that you put your mind to. Always dream big and never stop learning. The sky's the limit and I have no doubt that you'll continue to be a money mastermind after this book!

Kia Commodore
Author and Founder of Pennies to Pounds

GLOSSARY

AER (Annual Equivalent Rate) – sometimes called APR (annual percentage rate), this is the rate at which interest gets paid on savings or on money that you borrow

asset – an item or product that holds financial value

bankrupt – when a person or business is pronounced by law to be unable to pay back their debts

bitcoin – a cryptocurrency that was created in 2008

bond – when a government or company borrows money from investors with an agreed interest rate and time frame for repayment, in a form that can be bought through a similar process to opening a fixed term savings account

borrowing – taking money from a person or bank with an agreement to pay it back within a certain time frame

budget – a plan for your spending that includes your income, outgoings, savings, investments and debt

cashback – money given back on eligible purchases as a reward for shopping through particular bank accounts, credit cards or websites

CCJ (County Court Judgment) – a strike on your credit history when someone takes you to court because you owe them money and you haven't responded

chargeback – a payment protection scheme offered by some credit card companies that allows debit card customers to apply for a refund on purchases that are faulty or are not as described by the retailer

comparison shopping – comparing the price of a product between different retailers

compound interest – where interest owed or earned over the previous month or year is added to the total money you have saved or borrowed before the next interest calculation is made, so that interest is charged or owed on top of interest

Consumer Credit Act – legislation giving protection to consumers on credit and loan agreements (including spending with credit cards) that were made between the consumer and the retailer

contract – a legal agreement between two parties that details what both parties must deliver

credit – having an agreement to purchase an item or a service using borrowed money

credit card – a small plastic card (which can also be virtual) that is given to eligible consumers by a bank or financial institution to make purchases on credit

credit history – a record of all your credit searches, agreements and outstanding debt

credit score – a numerical summary of your borrowing history used by potential lenders to evaluate how responsible you are at borrowing money

cryptocurrency – a digital currency that can be used for online payments, but has no central regulation or backing (unlike the British Pound, which is backed by the Bank of England)

debit card – a small plastic card (which can also be virtual) that allows you to spend money directly from your bank account

debt – money that has been borrowed and has to be repaid

decentralised – when control is moved from a central entity (for example a bank) to a wider group of individuals or entities

deducted – taken away

default – a strike on your credit history when you fail to repay money borrowed, such as a loan or credit card payment

dividends – money paid out to shareholders from a company's profits

ETF (exchange traded fund) – an investment product that contains a variety of different assets (such as shares and bonds) and is traded on the stock exchange just like a share

fiat currency – a national currency that is issued and regulated by a government but is not backed by a physical asset such as gold or silver

fixed interest rate – an interest rate that does not change for a specified time

fraud – the crime of attempting to trick a victim for personal or financial gain

gambling – betting money on an event where the outcome is out of your control (for example a race) and is purely down to chance

HMRC (His Majesty's Revenue and Customs) – the UK government authority in charge of collecting taxes

income – money that you receive, for example from working

income tax – tax paid on income earned through employment once that amount is over the tax-free allowance threshold (also known as the personal allowance)

interest – money earned on savings or owed on money that you have borrowed

investing – putting money into assets with the hope that they will increase in value over time and provide a financial return

maintenance loan – the part of a student loan that covers living costs

money laundering – the crime of attempting to hide the origin of money gained illegally by transferring it through legal means such as overseas banks or a legitimate business

National Insurance number – a number given to UK residents over the age of 16 to help track your National Insurance contributions correctly

necessary spending – spending on things you must pay for, such as bills

negotiation – a discussion between two or more parties to reach a decision that both sides agree with

outgoings – also known as expenses or expenditure, this is money that you spend

overspending – spending more money than you can afford to

payday loan – a form of predatory lending that often comes with very high interest rates that make such loans unaffordable even in the short term

payslip – a document given to you by your employer each time you are paid that details your pay and any deductions that have been made such as tax, National Insurance and pension contributions

personal allowance – the value of earnings that an individual is able to earn before paying tax on their income

personal pension – a pension scheme that you invest in yourself, with no outside input

158

publicly traded companies – companies that offer part ownership of their companies as shares that are sold to investors on the stock market

purchase protection – protection offered to consumers at different levels depending on the method of payment used, which covers the cost of eligible items if they are stolen or damaged soon after you have bought them

renegotiation – to hold a discussion to decide new terms relating to a previous agreement

risk appetite – how much risk an investor is prepared to take with their investments

savings – money set aside for a specific goal or purpose or possible future need, such as a car, house or emergency fund

shareholder – someone who is a part-owner of a company by owning a share or shares

shares – equal parts of a company that people can own, which can be publicly traded on the stock market

spoofing – the act of trying to trick someone by pretending to be someone or something else, for example a bank

State Pension – the allowance given by the government to people over a certain age who have been paying National Insurance contributions for the required number of years

statutory rights – your legal rights as a consumer, over and above a retailer's individual policy

stock market – the general activity of buying stocks and shares, and the people and institutions that organise it

student loan – a low-interest loan given to students by the government via the Student Loans Company to cover the cost of tuition fees and living costs as a student

variable interest rate – an interest rate that may change over time

workplace pension – a pension scheme to which your employer contributes alongside your personal contributions (which are normally deducted from your pay automatically), starting once you're over the age of 22 and earning more than £10,000 a year

ABOUT THE AUTHOR

Kia Commodore is a financial expert who founded the Pennies to Pounds platform to empower young people through financial education. In August 2022, Kia starred in the Channel 4 series *Money on my Mind* and has appeared on BBC Newsnight and Scotland Tonight. Kia hosted Legal & General's podcast *A Little Bit Richer*, as well as co-hosting the BBC 5 Live podcast *Your Work, Your Money*. Her work has also been featured in The Guardian, The Sun, Cosmopolitan and The Huffington Post. *How to Handle Money* is her first book.

To find out more about Kia's work, visit her online at:
penniestopounds.co.uk | @penniestopounds